How I Became a Millionaire at 30!™

A Spiritual guide to unlock the door to Financial Prosperity, Debt Free Living and a Life Free of Stress, Worry and Anxiety.

Jonathan Edison, M.Ed.

J.E.E Publishing

ISBN 0-9740713-0-7

J E E Publishing

INTRODUCTION

Many people may read this book and have the preconceived notion that if they have already reached their thirtieth birthday, the information in this book will not be of any value.

NOT TRUE!

This book is designed in a vigorous and universal approach to empower every individual, regardless of Age to achieve everything that life has to offer. The only prerequisite required for achieving maximum wealth is that the reader of this book has to be an individual that is sick and tired, of being sick and tired, of being broke, stressed out, head over hills in debt and panic stricken when bills arrive in the mail. If this describes you, then don't feel bad, you're not alone. Millions of Americans across the country have the exact same feelings.

The good news is, if you're an individual that is willing to make a cold, calculated, conscious decision about Financial Freedom, Wealth and Stress Free Living, then regardless of your current position in life, I am happy to let you in on a little secret.

You have the Blue Print in your hands right now!

The 8 principles, outlined in chapters 8-10, will show you how to accumulate Millions of dollars, cancel credit card debt, repair your credit, cut your house note by 50% and live a Millionaires lifestyle, free of stress and anxiety.

I must warn you though, in achieving your goal of becoming completely debt free and swimming in Millions is going to require a driving desire, lots of energy, patience, prayer, love, boldness, fearlessness and dedication.
* Magic Wand sold separately (AAA batteries not included).

I apologize, if you were under the impression that there is a secret, a magic trick or some sort of gimmick to becoming a Millionaire by 30. A true Millionaire knows that **you cannot cheat the process!** Therefore, I apologize again for not including any lucky pick numbers, dream book references, or the Psychic hot line emergency assistance numbers. The reason, the odds of gaining financial wealth and freedom through these means are astronomical. If you use the 8 simple principles, I have furnished in this book, you will realize and learn that Millionaires are created everyday through wisdom, prayer and a little bit of elbow grease. Now, before you take your hard earned wages for the week and run down to your local casino and hit the slots, remember, Millionaires don't gamble, they take calculated risks. Gambling is a diseased hazardous adventure that can cause you financial ruin, stress and in some cases end in suicide.

A calculated risk taken by a Millionaire is a step-by-step manifested dream. A dream that has been devised into a plan, put into action, in turn, attracts and achieves wealth beyond belief.

This Book is Dedicated in The
Loving Memory of my Late
Grandmother Cloraine M. Turner.
I Will Always Love You Granny

Your Grandson,
John-John

FOREWORD

When he enters a room, you can feel his presence. He exudes a positive energy by the way he carries himself that says he has something special. The magnetism of his personality and the intensity in his voice brings out the best in you. With his head up, shoulders square and moving with a sense of purpose and urgency, you know right away he is a man of destiny and on a mission to change the world. As much as he has chosen this path for himself, it has chosen him.

Born in poverty to parents, one hooked on drugs and the other addicted to the streets, Jonathan Edison started out in life on the bottom looking down. Any casual observers waging bets against his chances of making it would have lost big time. Jonathan's still unfolding life story demonstrates there is nothing as powerful as a made up mind. Driven by the desire to keep the promise he made to his grandmother and shocked into reality by a close encounter with death, Jonathan set out to achieve what many would say was the impossible dream — financial wealth in the midst of failure and hopelessness. Armed with only a 1.6 grade point average, coupled with a fierce sense of focus, discipline and a thirst for knowledge, Jonathan rose from remedial classes to academic excellence, from bus attendant to the youngest person to reach his position in the history of the Michigan public school system.

From highly acclaimed educator to entrepreneur, author and nationally recognized speaker and business consultant, Jonathan hasn't even hit second gear yet. The pages of his story are revealing, raw, and riveting. Needless to say, life for Jonathan has not been a crystal stair. It has been good, bad and ugly. Dexter Yeager once said, "No test, no testimony." The testimony of Jonathan's life of accomplishment, in this book on how he rose from poverty to power, will inspire all of us to develop our millionaire potential and live life on a larger scale.

His message and insights are simple, yet very effective. His approach and advice are common sense, yet not common practice. Given what he had to overcome, Jonathan removes all excuses for us not doing more and achieving more. He proves unquestionably that it is not where you start out, it is where you are going. It is not what happens to you, it is what happens in you.

Jonathan has demonstrated we all have the capacity to earn millions and to create a life that most people only dream about. He says, "there is a millionaire in you." Pulling from his life experiences, Jonathan gives you the secret keys to uncover that millionaire and unlock a life of purpose, health and happiness. There is no question you will find your story in Jonathan's story and you will hear the still small voice within you say "If he can do it, I can do it." Read on and I guarantee you your life will never be the same again. Jonathan, you done me proud.

LES BROWN
The Motivator

ACKNOWLEDGEMENTS

I want to express that without the love, protection, grace and mercy of Almighty God, there would be no me. God is my strength and my rock. He has provided me with all of the wisdom, talents and gifts that I possess to do everything that I do. It is through Him that I am able to influence the lives of Millions in a positive way.

I also want to express my gratitude to several men in my life, who are champions and warriors in this universe. These men give me the inspiration and the encouragement to see far beyond my natural, spiritual and physical capabilities: Larry Edison, my father and the best friend a son could ever ask for. My pastor and spiritual father, Bishop Keith A. Butler, from Word of Faith International Christian Center. My mentor, LaVan Hawkins, CEO of LaVan Hawkins Food Group, Mike Quick and Bobby Johnson, Police Athletic League (P.A.L.) basketball coach's. Mr. Clyde Lewers, my fifth grade homeroom teacher, my family barber, Mr. Leroy Jackson, and my cousin, the late great Ricky Wilson, R.I.P. We love you.

These men have made a permanent imprint on my life that will never fade or diminish.

Men, if I am you, and you are me,
I am definitely destined for greatness.

Much Love

To the Mothers of Greatness

I would be remiss, if I didn't give thanks and appreciation to the women who have given me the insight, help, protection, love and prayers that have created the MAN that I am today. My mother (my hero), Glenda Horner, Ms. Angela Jordan, Mrs. Annie L. Hubbard, Mrs. Rosalind M. Butler, Pamela Jackson, Ph.D., Ms. Pat Hayes, Ms. Phyllis Coan, Ms. Carla Stamps, Ms. Karen Clingman, Phoebe Manister, Ph.D., Quanda L. Simmons, D.D.S., Kamilah M. Woodson, Ph.D., Ms. Lorraine Colts, Ms. Bridgess, and all the ladies of the Detroit Public School Center Building who have helped me realize my dream.

Ladies, I Love You
Your Son, Jonathan E. Edison

A Personal Letter From the Author

Dear Top Achiever,

I would like to thank you and say congratulations to you for making the commitment to yourself to make positive steps toward a happier and more fulfilled you. I believe that inspiration and motivation comes from within. But it is always the encouraging and inspiring stories of other individuals who have tested the water, overcome the defying odds and those who have snatched victory from the jaws of defeat that give us the courage to face our fears, to go upfront and take life head on. What does success mean to me? Success to me means doing what you believe in, doing what you love and doing what gives you great pleasure. It gives me great pleasure and honor to share my triumphant life story and my step-by-step formula for achieving maximum wealth with you.

However, I must warn you, if you're looking for a story of me clicking my heels three times, or a story of how God came to me in a dream and gave me the winning numbers for the power ball, sorry my friend, you're barking up the wrong tree. But, if you're looking for "real life" courage building principles, proven strategies to overcome fear and poverty, then take a look inside. Discover the life of an imperfect, flawed, mistake making, issue having young man who has overcome the negativity and the obstacles of the universe to become extremely successful. You have purchased the right blue print. I believe that anyone can reach his or her full and maximum potential through prayer, hard work and an overwhelming passionate desire to acquire the things that you subconsciously and consciously believe that life owes you. I hope you will enjoy this book, I look forward to speaking with you personally, chatting with you online, visiting with you in your living room or at your next book club meeting. Remember, you don't get in life what you deserve; you get in life what you are willing to sacrifice and work hard for. I thank God for all of the talents, gifts and grace, He has bestowed upon me. I now understand that God's protection over my life was a divine plan to use me as a tool to shape and inspire Millions who have fallen away from him. I really appreciate you allowing me the opportunity to be apart of you taking your life to the next level. I don't know about you, but I'm ready. Let's get it baby!

> *"Failure is not final. It's only a*
> *break in the action to clear your*
> *mind, get focused and come back*
> *even stronger."*
> — Jonathan Edison

CHAPTER ONE

A Golden Opportunity To
Give Up!
(The Boy)

Whannnnnnnnnn, "It's a boy!" September 8, a child was born to the parents of Larry and Glenda of Detroit, Michigan. Into what most statisticians and census bureau surveyors would consider the typical or ideal Black-American household. Unlike most typical American households, we lacked many of the amenities that accompanied such a high and revered status. We were a family dependent on the government's welfare system, using creative budgeting and a lot of "robbing Peter to pay Paul" coping methods. In order for us to survive as a family, we made do with a little and made a lot out of nothing!

At age 4, I embarked on many two-mile long walks with my mother to the Food Stamp Office. We picked up our $205 worth of food stamps, powdered eggs, canned beef and several bags of farina cereal that was meant to last us through the entire month. The walking didn't bother me at all. In fact, I enjoyed it. I always thought of it as an adventure; however, this was an understatement. Given the path we had to walk, I don't think Indiana Jones would have made it through my neighborhood. Along the way, we passed burned out houses that junkies used for safe havens. Vacant lots contained weeds that stood taller in stature than me, as if it were wheat crops. Abandoned cars stripped, burned and left sitting on bricks like carnage in the great jungles of Africa.

We would also encounter the neighborhood bum, hanging out at the corner store asking for change. The funny thing about it was no matter what day it happened to be; he always needed the same amount of money to "get him something to eat." It seemed as though the closer we got to the Food Stamp Office, the more eventful our trip became. We took a shortcut through a well-traveled field, because of its direct route to the Food Stamp Office. While approaching it, I could see from a distance the street hustlers, single mothers and even some elderly people buying and selling food stamps like they were trading shares of stock on Wall Street.

Standing in line, waiting patiently with my mother, I was always amazed at the amount of networking that took place. Deals were being made left and right. I watched the single mothers with as many as five or six children, crying and grabbing at them, while they negotiated to sell their hundreds of dollars worth of stamps for mere pennies on the dollar. My mom was often approached to sell her food stamps, but she always refused. She would simply say in a soft voice, "No, thank you. My little boy has to eat, look at how big his head is. I'd better keep some food in the house." The potential buyer would laugh and look down at me with my eyes as bright as the California sunshine and say, "You're right, baby. This boy is growing, you two be careful out here."

It was amazing to see the number of people who were dependent on these little white, green and red books that contained something that looked like Monopoly money. We exited the Food Stamp Office after receiving our books of food stamps and monthly rations of food. My mother would always make sure I had something to carry. This was something I looked forward to; it gave me the freedom of not holding her hand like a little baby. I felt I was a big boy. After she gave me my two bags of groceries, she would always ask, if they were too heavy. My reply was always the same, "No,

3

Mama, I got it. Let's go. I'm ready." As we began our trek back to the trail and through the shortcut, I would whistle, skip and play superhero. I was *He-man, a.k.a. John-John*, the "Master of the Ghetto."

I really enjoyed helping my mother with those bags of food. She'd always call me her *big boy* and I would say, "That's right, Mama, because big boys are strong." As we walked that long two-mile walk back to our house, my little arms and legs would get tired. She would ask me if I wanted to stop and rest. How could the "Master of the Ghetto" be tired? Under no condition would I stop walking. I wouldn't put my bags down because that would mean I wasn't a big boy in her eyes and that's the last thing I wanted.

My parents and I lived with my grandmother in a small two-family flat on Detroit's eastside in the heart of what was known as "Black Bottom" by most people who lived in the community. It was an area of Detroit that most of the elite or middle class looked down on because of the violence, the prostitution and the drug trafficking that occurred in the neighborhood. Our home sat between two vacant lots, which seemed to be the headquarters for the rodents that took up residence during the bitter cold winter months. Although we were poor, broke and living in the ghetto with a terrible infestation problem, we had two things that a lot of families in my neighborhood didn't possess. There was love and stability in our home. At least I thought there was.

For me, life as a child couldn't get any better. I had my mom, my dad, and the most loving grandmother in the world to nurture, train and care for me. This was rare because the perfect family structure in the Black Community was just as non-existent as the Millionaire living next door. Considering the amount of love my mother expressed for my father, our family and me, I found it very difficult to understand how one individual could create such hell, cause so much destruction and ultimately serve as the instrumental force in destroying my happy family, my home and my relationship with my mother.

His name was Donovan. He was my mother's first true love from high school. He was also the father of my mother's first two children, Marshall and Laurie, my older brother and sister. Donovan was a tall, smooth-talking man with deep hazel eyes, bronze toned-skin, perfect model-type bone structure, and jet-black wavy hair, which he wore in a pony-tail that the Great Sampson himself would envy. In the late 60's and early 70's, he was considered by most women to be the Clark Gable of the ghetto. Although my mother seemed to love my father with all of her heart, it didn't erase the fact that Donovan was her first true love. Donovan's hold on my mother ran deep into her very soul. She found it virtually impossible to say no to him. It was as though he controlled her very will, her emotions and her actions with his magnetic personality, winning smile and mouth-watering beauty.

Donovan lived a fast life. He loved drugs, alcohol, living life on the edge, and stealing from others. He majored in car and merchandising theft. He stole from parking lots and large warehouses. His minor was petty theft, pedaling cheap drugs and looking for his next innocent victim. Donovan spent the majority of his time in jail, plotting ways to super-impose his chosen life style on my mother.

The Beginning of the End

"Glenda, I'm missing $50 out of my wallet. Have you seen it?" my father asked my mother while getting dressed for his 7:00 a.m. shift at the plant. "No honey, what $50? Maybe you spent it or it fell out of your wallet!" she said.

My father didn't protest. He just left for work with a look of bewilderment on his face. Little did my father know that my mother had used the $50 to bail Donovan out of jail the night before, while he was at work on his afternoon job.

As the weeks went on, it was obvious that my mother's mind was elsewhere. She wasn't the same energetic and vibrant mother I knew. She seemed to be really tired all the time. She even had trouble staying focused and keeping her head up. On this particular morning, as she attempted to make pancakes for the entire family, something was wrong. It was as if she had fallen asleep standing up over the hot stove. The pancakes burned and the entire kitchen instantly filled with smoke. I just sat at our small two-chair kitchenette and cried when my father and grandmother started yelling at her. "What the hell is wrong with you? Are you high on something?" they yelled. Although they were being facetious and yelling out of fear, their remarks were valid. She was high on something all right! Donovan's love and the pills he provided for her. My father opened the back door to let the smoke escape from the kitchen. My mother didn't respond. She just stood there with a blank look on her face and a glaze in her eyes that stripped her charismatic personality.

Gradually, my mother's condition worsened. This was due to the amount of time she spent away from home. My dad worked two minimum-wage jobs to support the family and my mother's full time job was spending as much quality time she could with Donovan behind my father's back. During the day, my mother would return home reeking of cheap liquor on her breath and the strong odor of cigarettes in her clothes. Within a few weeks, my mother's new behavior became more and more apparent. My grandmother, even in her elderly state, began to notice a change in my mother's demeanor and attitude.

"Glenda, child, do you need some help? I'm worried about you girl. You don't look so good," she said.

My mother exclaimed that she was fine. She was just under a lot of pressure lately. As I sat in my room playing marbles on the floor, the pressure of trying to hide her love for Donovan was too much for her to bare. Suddenly, out of nowhere, she yelled.

"JUST LEAVE ME ALONE! JUST LEAVE ME ALONE! I'M SICK AND TIRED OF EVERYONE ASKING ME IF I'M ALL RIGHT! I'M SICK OF THIS HOUSE, I'M SICK OF CLEANING, I'M SICK OF COOKING, I'M SICK OF THAT BAD ASS BOY RUNNING ALL AROUND THE HOUSE, I'M SICK OF YOUR OLD ASS, AND I'M SICK AND TIRED OF BEING, SICK AND TIRED!"

I had never heard my mother talk like that before. What could this mean? She didn't love me anymore? Was I a bad kid? It's my fault, I thought as I blamed myself. Immediately, I dropped all of my marbles and ran to the door in my Incredible Hulk pajamas screaming and crying, "Mama, I'm sorry. Mama, I'm sorry. I promise, I'll be a good boy. I promise, Mama, I'll be good." My mother collapsed on the floor from exhaustion and grief. I sat next to her, stroking her hair ever so gently. I said, "Mama, don't be sad, I'm going to be a big boy and help you, okay?" She looked at me with tears in her eyes, held me tight and kissed my forehead as a loving mother would do and said, "Okay, you be a big boy and help your mama."

Shortly after my mother's emotional explosion, my father came home from his second job. At 1:00 a.m. in the morning, he began to question her whereabouts. My father also questioned her strange behavior and her seemingly lack of attention towards him and our family. In my bedroom, behind the closed door, I could hear my parents arguing faintly from a distance. And, like every curious six-year-old, I attempted to get a closer seat to the action. I watched and listened to my parents argue for several hours from the keyhole of their bedroom door. My dad asked her where she was during the day, while I was attending school. He also questioned her about the strange phone calls we were receiving in the middle of the night. My mom made excuse after excuse, but none of them added up to a sum that satisfied my father's search for the truth. My father was no fool. He knew exactly what was going on. He just wanted my mother to be honest with him in the name of love.

It had become common knowledge that Donovan was out of jail and hot on the trail of my mother to claim her as his "Bonnie" as he continued with his crime spree throughout the community. My mother's relationship with Donovan became more intense as the days went by. They were sneaking around drinking and partying, while Donovan provided my mother with hundreds of pills, which she used to intoxicate herself each week. As the constant alcohol and drug abuse continued, my grandmother did everything she could to protect and keep me in the dark about my mother, Donovan, and their drug habit. My mother's relationship with Donovan progressed from casually hanging out, drinking, and drug use during the day into two-week excursions. They bounced from house to house and hotel to motel. Although my dad pretended to be unaffected by the turn of events in our household, it was destroying him inside. My mother's behavior and bad choices were destroying the very foundation of our happy home.

The final straw for my dad was the day my mother's abuse to herself turned into physical abuse for me. One day, while my dad was at work and my grandmother was sleeping, my mom decided to have a continental breakfast of pills and a 32 oz. bottle of Pink Champale to wash them down with. This day just happened to be the first Saturday of the month. The day I looked forward to, the day we went on our adventure. She came in my room at 7:00 a.m. in the morning and said, "Come on, John-John. Get ready, we're going to pick up our food stamps." Ordinarily, I would have sprung out of bed, but my mother didn't look very well. Ten minutes later, she returned.

She said, "Com on boy, it'sss time to go, we don't want to be late. So get dweessed and huuurry up, damm it!"

Why was Mama talking funny? Was she alright? Maybe she's just sleepy, as she always appeared to be lately, I thought to myself. After the exhausting two-mile walk to the Food Stamp Office, my mother could barely keep her head up.

She said, "Baby, give Mama a few minutes and we can go, okay?" as she sat on the curb outside the Food Stamp Office. I complied and sat with her. Strangers walked by us staring at my mother, shaking their heads saying things like, "Look at her, she's high as hell." What did this mean, "high as hell?" I thought.

"Mama, are you okay? I'm ready to go! Come on, Mama, let's go! I'm ready to play superhero and be the "Master of the Ghetto," I said.

"Alright, baby, we can go," she said.

As she stood to her feet, I noticed her swaying from side to side. She managed to get herself together long enough to make it to the corner store. While my mother paced the aisles of the store, I wanted to get a sneak peak at my favorite superheroes and the possible opportunity to sneak and open a tasty bag of *Andy Capps Hot Fries* potato chips. My mother turned to me and asked if I wanted something. I responded, "Yes, ma'am. I want these hot fries I found opened on this rack," I exclaimed with crumbs of chips all around my lips and in my mouth.

"Alright, boy, you think you're so smart, don't you?" she said, as she paid the clerk for the items she had placed on the counter with my bag of chips. During the brief moment it took the clerk to bag up my mother's groceries, the next minute of my life changed my appearance forever. As we turned to exit the store, there he was: the most stunning man I had ever laid eyes on. He was handsome, standing in the doorway with a tank top on, showing off his rippling muscles and smooth chest hairs. Finally, I was face to face with the man who was destroying my family, Donovan.

"Glenda, is that you?" he asked. My mother stopped in her tracks, she was mesmerized by this man's presence. I just couldn't stop looking at him. He looked as if he should have been on the side of my Superfriends lunch box, posing as one of the new superheroes.

"How are you doing, little boy?" he asked me.

"I'm not a little boy. I'm a big boy, right Mama?" I said.

I looked back to get her approval. She didn't hear me. Her mind was in the very soul of Donovan's nature. "Mama, let's go. Mama, let's go. Mama, I'm ready to go!" I shouted, as I pulled her hand. In haste, my mother gathered up our things and rushed to the door. But there was one problem: the sleeve of my jacket was caught on the potato chip rack. With my hand locked in hers, she didn't notice that I was caught.

Fresh out of her hypnotic trance and in a rush to keep me away from the man she was secretly in love with, she jerked repeatedly. The last time was one time too many. I yelled for her to stop, but my cry went unnoticed. I hit the concrete floor and let out a scream that would have drowned out a national tornado warning alert. Crash! My mother quickly dropped all of her groceries when she heard me in distress. That very moment, she cried, "OH MY GOD! SOMEBODY CALL AN AMBULANCE! MY BABY IS HURT! MY BABY IS HURT!" Instantly, blood gushed out of my head onto the cold concrete floor. Mass hysteria took place as everyone attempted to provide me with some sort of medical attention. The store clerk quickly grabbed towels from his storeroom to try and stop the bleeding. The other patrons in the store held my hand and continuously whispered in my ear, "You're going to be alright, little man, you're going to be alright." Still in shock from the incident, Donovan just stared at my mother as she tried her best to comfort and console her injured son.

After several minutes of complete pandemonium, we could hear an ambulance approaching in the distance with its sirens blaring. The Emergency Medical Team rushed into the store and whisked me off into the ambulance with a course set for Children's Hospital. My mother's eyes were blood-shot from crying as she gazed over me, watching as I lay on the bed in the back of the ambulance bleeding from the right side of my head. The look in her eyes was so apologetic that she didn't have to say a word. The only thing I could think of at that moment was that I didn't know superheroes could bleed.

During the 15-minute ride to the emergency room, she must have said she was sorry over a thousand times. With tears in her eyes, the last thing she said to me as the Emergency Technicians wheeled me into the hospital was, "Baby, you're going to be fine and Mama's going to be right here waiting on you, okay?" In a faint voice, weak from blood loss, I told her, "I know, Mama. Everything is going to be okay because I'm a big boy and big boys are strong." That afternoon at Children's Hospital, I received sixteen stitches to my right eyebrow. Thanks to the negligence of my mother and that no good Donovan.

The following day, my grandmother decided she couldn't tolerate any more foolishness from my mother. She was not going to sit by and watch my mother destroy her son and grandson's life in one big swoop. I sat on my bed in pain from the fresh stitches in my head and listened to my grandmother and mother argue back and forth about her condition, her parenting skills and how my grandmother didn't have any right to butt into her personal business. My mother professed that she was grown, free and knew how to take care of her own son. The more my mother pretended to be fine, the more her drug and alcohol abuse was continuing to spiral out of control. My father pleaded with her to get herself cleaned up for the sake of our family, but his pleas were useless. She became a slave to Donovan's pills and alcohol.

By age six and a half, I had become numb to the constant fighting, arguing and yelling that seemed to lead to my mother's disappearance for weeks at a time. Even through all of the hardships, sleepless nights and pain I suffered emotionally, I still managed to be a pretty decent student in school. I realize now the reason I never cared for missing school or even being late: I was trying to escape the reality of a negative situation in my home life. Even as a child, I knew something wasn't right and I yearned for a sense of security and stability. The reality had set in, my family was falling apart and I couldn't do a thing to prevent it. I couldn't control it and I couldn't stop it. Even with all of my superhero powers, this was too much for the "Master of the Ghetto" to contend with. As my mother popped in and out of my life, sometimes she managed to take me to school when my grandmother wasn't feeling up to the challenge.

This particular bright sunny morning, my mother seemed to be in good spirits, sober to the best of my knowledge. She convinced my grandmother that she was doing okay, which meant she was free of any pills, alcohol or mind-altering drugs that would impair her from making proper decisions. That morning, she made breakfast the way she used to. Pancakes, eggs, sausage, freshly squeezed orange juice and plenty of syrup. Could it be that my mother was back from the dead? I wondered. I didn't know, but I liked the new her. "Hurry up and get ready for school. I know how you hate to be late," she said. I got myself ready for a brand new day of learning, interacting with my friends and my favorite class, gym. Bump! Bump!

"There's our cab, John-John. Come on, let's go!" Mama said.

"I thought we were walking, Mama," I replied.

"Well son, Mama has to make a quick stop first, then I'm going to drop you off at school, okay? It will only take a few minutes, I promise."

The cab sped off and headed down the main road for about twenty minutes, then the driver made a sharp left turn onto what appeared to be an alley. As the tires rolled over the potholes, it caused me to shake in the cab. I noticed a lot of tall burned-out buildings on both my left and right side. All of the buildings seemed to have some type of debris in front of them. Some had huge trucks, some had flocks of pigeons and pigeon droppings completely covering everything and some were completely boarded up. Once the cab came to a complete stop, my mother paid the driver and we jumped out. As soon as she opened the door, the vile smell of the slaughterhouse, burning trash from the incinerator and the fumes from all of the trucks gave us a huge kiss in the mouth and nose.

My mother started walking towards a warehouse that looked totally condemned. Most of the windows were broken out, the back half was burned to a crisp and you could hear water dripping all the way through it. I followed close behind her with my hands in my pocket because I didn't want to touch anything. My mother started scaling the fire escape like Catwoman herself, purring all the way up to the third level. As I climbed up behind her, I wondered where we were going because I didn't see any doors.

Once we got to the third level, she picked me up and shoved me through an opening that was formally a complete window. I fell on the floor next to a pregnant bucket of human feces and urine that smelled like dead bodies. The stench was disgusting. I vomited all over the cold wooden floor and most of my shirt. After my mother came through the opening, she picked me up, wiped my mouth and told me to go play. As I walked through this one room of horror, I saw pigeons in the ceiling doing their business all over the place. There were also large rat droppings all over the floor. The floor itself was broken and rotted out, which made it very easy to see down to the second and first level of the warehouse. There weren't any lights, electricity, appliances or furniture in the entire place. The only thing to sit on was a twin sized mattress with no sheets on it. It had more urine stains on it than a hundred baby diapers. Even in the day-time, this place was still cold and dark. I felt like we were in Dracula's first apartment and he was subleasing. After I checked everything out, I stood in the corner with my mouth covered to protect myself from the odor and fumes.

When I reached down to tie my shoe, to my surprise, there he was again. Just as I had remembered, the day at the corner store. Only this time, he didn't have the same twinkle in his eye and his very existence didn't intimidate or engulf me as it had during our first encounter. His demeanor was that of a man who was nervous, unsure of himself and desperate.

"Glenda! What took you so damn long? And why do you have this big head ass boy with you?" he asked.

"Well, I had to pretend to be taking him to school, so I could make sure I had enough time to steal the money from his daddy to get high with."

My mother and Donovan had the money they needed. Donovan left for about half an hour and returned with all the pills and liquor they could buy with the money they had. I was now close to an hour late for school and my patience was

14

growing thin. "Mama, I'm ready to go. Mama, I'm ready to go to school, Mama!" I yelled. I turned the corner and witnessed my mother gobbling down pills and drinking Pink Champale as if it were manna from heaven. As our eyes met, she said to me, "I better not ever catch you doing this. This is not good for you. You hear me talking to you, boy?" "Yes, Mama," I said, standing in shock as Donovan ran his hands over my mother's body in places that were considered to be private.

Finally, two hours later, the party was over. Donovan went outside and hailed a cab and sent us on our way. During the cab ride, I couldn't look at my mother. I just stared out the window, looking into the sky, leaning my head against the door of the cab and listening to my mother babble on and on in her drunken condition. I wondered if my mother would ever get better. I was sad, scared and confused but I knew I had to be a big boy.

We arrived in front of the school almost three hours late. My teacher could see from the window adjacent to her desk that my mother and I were having some difficulty outside. Not me, but my mother. She was so stoned that she couldn't hold her head up. Her legs were like rubber and she was cursing everything from airports to zippers. My second grade teacher ran to assist her but my mother refused. "Jonathan, go on in and take your seat. I'll be there in a few minutes," she told me. Reluctantly, I followed her instructions, but intrinsically I knew it was the best advice. Once inside, I hung up my coat and watched from the front door of the school. My teacher struggled to help my mother back into the cab. Unfortunately, the tussle concluded with my mother vomiting all over my teacher's shiny black patent leather shoes. Now exhausted and humiliated, my teacher proceeded back inside.

Standing in the front door, I was in tears, ashamed of

15

what had just happened. My teacher said to me, "Jonathan, don't worry about that. You're a smart boy." As we walked down the hallway of the school, several of the other teachers had made their way into the corridor. In the doorway, only a few feet from my desk, I overheard my teacher whispering to another teacher under her breath, "It's a shame, this boy is going to end up on drugs, dead or in jail."

That afternoon, the principal called my house to inform my grandmother of what had transpired that morning between my mother and my teacher. The principal explained how he felt it was in the best interest of my safety and the safety of others that my mother not be allowed to pick me up or drop me off anymore. After little convincing, my grandmother agreed. She called my dad at work and explained to him what had happened. At 3:30 p.m. that afternoon, my dad picked me up from school. With deep sadness on his face he said, "How's my boy? How was school today? Tell me what you learned today?" As I proceeded with my answers, he quickly replied, "Oh, you're so smart." Through my dad's own personal pain and disappointment, he still managed to build me up. His heart was broken because his family was falling apart and his son was in the middle of a whirlwind that was out of control.

That night when my dad came home from work, he woke my mother up out of her drunken stupor and broke the bad news to her. He informed her that it wasn't a good idea for her to pick me up or drop me off at school anymore. Immediately, my mother became irate. She started throwing things, yelling obscenities and screaming that no one had the right to keep her from taking me to school. As the yelling began, I covered my head with both of my pillows and curled up into a perfectly tight ball to try and drown out the sound of their voices, but it didn't work. Back and forth they argued, which felt like days.

Suddenly it stopped. I jumped out of the bed and peeked through my door. I could barely make out the image, but it looked as if my mother was lying on the floor face down. I ran over to her as fast as my little feet could carry me. "Mama, get up! Mama, please get up!" I cried. My father had reached his limit. He couldn't deal with it anymore. In the midst of the argument, before he knew it, he had pushed my mother down on the living room floor. "That's it! Don't no man put his hands on me!" she screamed, as she rose to her feet. I began to cry. I didn't know what was happening, but I knew it wasn't right. I didn't want her to go, but she immediately ran to their bedroom and started shoving her things in a large black Hefty bag. I ran into my parent's bedroom after her and pleaded with her not to leave. Somehow I thought all of this commotion was my fault.

I shouted, "MAMA, PLEASE DON'T GO! MAMA, PLEASE DON'T GO, I PROMISE I'LL BE GOOD. I PROMISE I'LL BE A BIG BOY AND DON'T CRY! MAMA, PLEASE!"

As she stormed down the steps with her black Hefty bag over her shoulder, she said, "Don't you worry, John-John. It's going to be okay. Mama will be back for you, baby, real soon. I promise!" This was the worst day of my young life. Everyone was crying and my mother was gone. Worst of all, I blamed myself for everything that happened.

After that day, my life would never be the same again. The sun rose early the next day. I could hear the birds chirping through the window from my bedroom. At 6 a.m. my mother, Donovan, and two of his biker friends showed up at our house on a mission to rescue me from the clutches of my father and evil grandmother. Their motive was obvious, without me, my mother couldn't receive her food stamps or monthly ration of food. Therefore, in Donovan's eyes, I was the goose that laid the golden egg to help supply the funds for his crime spree and drug habit. Somehow, my mother had managed to sneak her way into the house and into my bedroom undetected by anyone.

I thought I was dreaming when she whispered in my ear, "John-John, John-John, wakeup, wakeup, baby." Soon I realized it was no dream when I felt my mother's warm breath on the side of my face. I slowly opened my eyes and there she was standing over me with my jacket in her hand whispering, "Baby, come on, let's go. Mama is taking you with her." But, a trip to the bathroom by my grandmother spoiled my mother's plan. She noticed the front door opened and a black Chevy van parked right outside our door. She knew immediately what was going on. "ED, ED, GET UP!" she shouted, "GLENDA IS TRYING TO KIDNAP JOHN-JOHN!"

My father sprang from his bed, ran across the hall and forced the door open. In disbelief, he witnessed my mother as she attempted to pack my clothes and leave our home to take me with her. He told her she had five seconds to drop my clothes and leave our home before he called the police. "Leave now, Glenda! I mean it! You need to leave now! John is not going with you under any condition. So get out for the last time!" As my dad tried to remove my mother from my room, she began to scream. Suddenly, a voice from a distance came barreling up the stairs.

"Glenda, are you alright? Do you need me to come up there?" That's right. It was the man, the myth, the legendary Donovan himself on our front porch, yelling up the stairs to rescue my mother. Like a strong gust of Chicago wind, my father flew from my room to the front door where he heard this strange man's voice beckoning for my mother. In rage, unbelief and brokenheartedness, my father made eye contact with Donovan in the hallway on the stairs, which led up to our front door. In the next moment, as if God Himself had cracked the sky to speak from heaven.

My father yelled, "IF YOU DON'T WANT TO DIE

TODAY, YOU BETTER GET THE HELL AWAY FROM MY DOOR RIGHT NOW!" Then he said to my mother, "You have the nerve to bring this gangster to my house to steal my son. I swear, if you don't get the hell out of here right now, someone is going to get hurt and I promise you, I won't be the last one!"

The air was thick and filled with fear and tension. My mother was very adamant on taking me with her even after my father's thunderous threat to Donovan. She gathered up as many of my clothes as she could and snatched me out of bed with a mission of escape on her mind. Wearing my Incredible Hulk pajamas and no socks, I stood watching my mother as she peeked out at my father who was still blocking the front door. With my clothes in one hand and me tightly nestled by her side in the other, my mother built up enough courage to make a move for the door. But in all the commotion, instead of running, she just casually strolled through the hallway like nothing was going on. My grandmother armed with her cane made of solid oak wood met us near the kitchen.

"Glenda, I'm telling you right now, you'd better let my grandbaby go or I'm going upside your head so hard with this cane that my new middle name is going to be "Hit 'em Hard Hoe!" I don't want to hurt you, Glenda, so just let him go! He doesn't belong to you and he's not going with you!" My mother in her distorted state began to shriek and yell, "I'm taking my baby with me no matter what anybody says or does! He's my son and he belongs to me!"

With so many emotions running through my little mind, I didn't know who to side with. I loved my mother and I wanted to go with her, but I knew she wasn't well. I loved my granny and I wanted to stay with her, but my granny and my mother where yelling and cursing at each other. I loved my father and I wanted to stay with him, but I could see in his eyes that he didn't love my mother anymore.

"Glenda, let him go! Let him go NOW!" my father yelled again.

"Hey man! Stop yelling at my woman! Glenda, get that boy and let's go!" Donovan yelled up the stairs.

The height of the standoff had reached its peak. Donovan was yelling, my mother was screaming, my father was in kill mode and my grandmother was ready for war. As I stood in the middle of this typhoon of anger, confusion, insanity and twisted love affair, I just closed my eyes. I shut everything out and pretended that I was on my journey to the Food Stamp Office on a bright Saturday morning. I was whistling, having fun and playing superhero, saving and protecting the ghetto from evildoers. All the shouting and the increased levels of hostility in my house soon interrupted my fantasy. My mother grew impatient and began to yell even louder, almost like a lioness in the jungle does to protect her cubs. Donovan's taunts began to burn inside my father's ears. My grandmother's cane was still cocked, locked and ready to rock at the drop of a dime.

Suddenly, my mother grabbed me tight, dropped my clothes and charged towards my father blocking the front door. My grandmother swung her cane, missing my mother by only inches. However, she managed to hit me in the top of the head with it. My father was furious at this point. With me tucked at her side, my mother tried her best Jim Brown move, but it didn't work on the 6'2", 250 lb., All-American athlete and former soldier. In one enormous swoop, my dad grabbed me out of my mother's arms, sending her in a spin. With me in one hand, he pushed her out of the door with the other. In a matter of seconds, she headed down the stairs. Lucky for her, Donovan was there to break her fall. However, my mother wasn't done by a long shot.

She charged back up the stairs after me. Before my father

could react, my mother lunged out and grabbed the bottom of my pajama pants. Without care or fear for his safety, Donovan ran up the stairs after my mother and assisted her in pulling me down the stairs with them. The mental torment for me during all of this was unbearable. Maybe it was the blow to the head or maybe it was just my nerves, but my physical body couldn't handle another ounce of pain. While my mother pulled at me with Donovan's help and my father and grandmother pulled at me to keep me in the house, it couldn't have been more than five minutes before I passed out from hysteria and my body went limp. At the end of the tug-of-war, my father and grandmother prevailed. My grandmother quickly shut and locked the door with the dead bolt.

Of course, my mother wasn't happy with the outcome of this battle. She took her protest to the street and stood outside yelling at the top of her lungs, how she loved me and how she was never going to leave me. Forty-five minutes later, Donovan decided enough was enough, then took my mother by the hand forcing her into the van. Once my mother was in the van, she proceeded to continue her rampage. "I'm coming back for my baby! I'm coming back for you! He's mine, he's mine!" she exclaimed, as they sped away in the van.

Hours later, I felt like I had been run over by a truck. My head was throbbing, my ankle was bruised and two of my fingers on my left hand were sprained. The pain I experienced during this episode was even more excruciating than when I split my head open in the store. As I lay on my bed in agonizing pain, I looked over to my dresser and caught a glimpse of my Superfriends lunch box, I thought to myself, "I'm getting out of the superhero business. It's too much pain involved." In the aftermath of what had taken place that morning, my house was pretty calm. My dad went to work as normal. My grandmother sat in the kitchen listening to the news on her small clock radio while she enjoyed her morning cup of coffee. We tried to pick up the pieces and move on with our lives. It was difficult for all of us, because my mother was an indispensable part of the puzzle that was missing and we missed her love.

As time went by, the love I had for my mother grew even stronger. My love for her was deep. Many nights, I lay awake and cried myself to sleep because I wanted to be near her. Who was going to walk with me to the Food Stamp Office now? Who was going to make my breakfast the way she did? For the next few months, I was completely emotionally unbalanced. After the incident in my living room, I developed a severe case of chronic bedwetting. As soon as I laid down and closed my eyes to go to sleep, I would wet myself. When it happened, I didn't know what was wrong with me. I tried to drink little or nothing before bedtime. Unfortunately, it did nothing to remedy the situation. I was too embarrassed to tell my father. What would he do, if he knew his only son was a bed-wetter? I could not confide in my grandmother either because I knew she would have definitely told my father. Initially, I tried the old *change the sheets and flip the mattress over early in the morning before anyone woke up* routine, but I was wetting the bed so much that my mattress, my room and my superhero pajamas began to reek of a strong urine odor.

After a week or so, my secret was discovered. My dad was getting ready for work, when he decided to come into my bedroom and go over my homework with me. When he opened the door, he found me butt-naked with my mattress in hand, standing in a pile of smelly sheets and pajamas. Surprisingly, he didn't get upset. He had a temper when it came to foolishness, but on this occasion he was very understanding. He stood in my doorway and told me to put the mattress down and tell him what was bothering me. I explained to him as plainly as a seven-year old could that I couldn't stop wetting my bed and I missed my mother. My father didn't say a word. He stood in silence, frozen in the doorway for about thirty seconds, which felt like thirty days to me. His eyes swelled with tears as the love he felt for my mother slowly rolled down his cheeks in tears. I glanced up at him in bewilderment. I'd never seen my father cry before. I didn't even know he could cry. To me, my father was invincible. I ran and jumped into his arms and he carried me to the bathroom. Then I got ready for school.

School was great, I loved my teacher, I loved my class and I really loved being one of the smartest kids in school. By the second semester of the third grade, I managed to make the honor roll. I had perfect attendance and I was never tardy. My grandmother and father were so proud of me. My bedwetting problem was at a minimum and I had a firm grip on who I was and how much love was still in my home. "Oh happy days they were!" I was big enough to walk to school by myself and had become somewhat of a celebrity for being the only kid in school with perfect attendance. The joke that preceded me was you could set your watch by me because I was always on time. This new found happiness and confidence that my father and grandmother worked so hard to instill in me came to a screeching halt when my mother and Donovan decided to invite themselves back into my life unannounced.

It was a normal Thursday afternoon, at Tendler Elementary School. At 2:45 p.m., my classmates and I were putting away our supplies and gathering up our things to get ready for the weekend. Ms. Thomas, my third grade teacher was busy passing out treats as she always did to the students who had good behavior that week. As I cleared my desk and put away my multiplication flash cards, the school secretary called down to my classroom over the intercom. *"Please excuse the interruption, Ms. Thomas. Can you send Jonathan Horner to the office. His parent is here to pick him up. He's going home."* Ms. Thomas gave me a treat and a hug then handed me three sheets of homework and sent me on my way. I ran to my locker and grabbed my jacket, my book-bag, then headed to the office. As I walked through the brightly lit hallways, I wondered who was picking me up early?

When I got to the office, I noticed a lady in a long black trench coat having a conversation with the secretary. The woman's voice sounded familiar, but I wasn't sure. As the mysterious woman dressed in all black turned around, she resembled my mother. My little eyes immediately began to glow with anticipation that it could be her. In a matter of seconds, we were face to face. It was my mother standing in the office, wearing dark sunglasses with a bag of *Andy Capps Hot Fries* potato chips in her hand. "Come on, baby, let's go home," she said, casually dangling the bag of chips in front of me. I was frozen in my tracks. I didn't know how to react. My grandmother had taught me not to talk to strangers, but she was not a stranger. She was the woman that gave birth to me. The woman that I took my long adventurous walks with. So many thoughts were dancing in my head: what I should do? I feared her, but I loved her. I didn't want to see her, but I missed her. I couldn't stand to be without her, so I went with her.

As we walked towards the front door of the school, she stopped, kneeled down and told me how much she loved me. She also said that she and my dad were back in love and he told her to pick me up. As odd as it sounded, I believed her.

I took her hand and we walked out of the school together.

We jumped in a waiting taxi. I was so excited at the idea of us being a happy family again! I couldn't wait to see the look on my father's face when he got home from work. With a smile as big as the Grand Canyon and the enthusiasm of a good Baptist Preacher, I turned to my mother and shouted, "I love you, Mama!" But, she didn't respond. She just rocked back and forth, staring out of the back of the window through her sunglasses. She seemed very nervous. She kept turning around looking through the back window as if somebody was after her.

I looked over at her again and yelled, "Mama, aren't you happy? Mama, aren't you happy? Come on, get happy, Mama!" Lucky for her, my teacher, Ms. Thomas, had us working on expressing ourselves that week in class. My mother snatched her dark sunglasses off her face and fired a response back to me that sent chills through my body.

"BOY, SHUT UP! SHUT UP FOR JUST ONE MINUTE, WILL YOU? I CAN'T THINK AND YOU'RE MAKING ME NERVOUS SO BE A GOOD BOY AND BE QUIET!"

In total shock and disappointment of my mother's response, I slowly turned away, slumped down in my seat and stared out the window. As the cab made its way through the city, I noticed that none of the scenery looked familiar to me. I immediately perked up.

I asked, "Mama, where are we going? This is not the way home."

She said, "Boy, didn't I tell you to be quiet? It's a surprise, okay? Now sit back, relax and SHUT UP!"

The further the driver drove, the more nervous I became. It became clear to me that our destination was not 2925 Lycaste where I lived. Suddenly, the cab made a sharp right turn onto a narrow street that began to look familiar to me. Tall old buildings surrounded us as we drove up the block. Immediately, I knew where we were going. It was the same place we had been the day I was late for school. As the cab pulled closer to the warehouse, fear consumed my entire body. I couldn't imagine that my mother would ever expose me to such an evil, disgusting and filthy place for a second time. But there we were again, making that same climb up the fire escape and through the window that led to HELL as I imagined it. The horrible smell of sewer sludge and rotting mildewed wood greeted us at the window. Once we were inside and I passed the first few puddles of water, my eyes began to tear up from the fumes. I went into a violent sneezing fit from the dust. Once I regained my composure and finally scanned the room, I noticed a sea of large boxes with pictures of 32-inch televisions on the side of them. The boxes took up most of the space in the warehouse.

I followed my mother as she maneuvered her way to a small area in the back, near an open window facing the street. I heard loud husky voices, as we approached the other room. That's right! It was Donovan and his two motorcycle buddies that tried to take me from my dad's house. Villains dressed in dark clothes and dark sunglasses; a job for the "Master of the Ghetto." I stood back and watched how they celebrated over a job well done. Earlier that morning, the three of them had broken into Fretter's Appliance store and cleaned them out. Donovan and his gang managed to get away with approximately forty 32-inch color television sets. After the celebration was over, Donovan approached me and extended his hand motioning for me to give him a high-five, but I just stared a hole through him like he was invisible. I was no longer in awe of him nor was I afraid of him, my mother, or anything else. I was only eight-years old and I had gone through the worst. My emotions and feelings had been seared out of me. At that very second with my heart pumping and my adrenaline on full throttle, I stood with my chest out and shouted at Donovan in his face, "YOU'D BETTER

TAKE ME HOME RIGHT NOW, PUNK! OR I'M GOING TO CALL MY FATHER AND YOU KNOW HE WILL COME AND KICK YOUR BUTT."

Donovan and his biker buddies thought my tirade was hilarious. They joked about me being tough enough to join their gang. But all of the laughter came to a halt, when I surprised Donovan with a technique my gym teacher taught us in school if a stranger tried to grab me or hurt me. I shot Donovan a straight right jab to his private parts so hard that I put him down on his knees. Silence fell over the entire room as I stood over Donovan waiting to hit him, if necessary. My mother couldn't believe what I had just done. She pushed me out of the way and immediately ran over to him. Extremely embarrassed, with tears of pain in his eyes, he stood up and started swearing and yelling at me, describing what he was going to do to me. I didn't care. I stood my ground and kept the wind to my back. I was a BIG BOY now and I was being strong like my mother had taught me to be.

Once the commotion settled down, I noticed that it was dark outside and I could smell rain in the air. I told my mother that I wanted to go home, but my cries fell on deaf ears. As darkness, rain and hunger set in, I felt desperate. I sat in a corner of the warehouse and watched Donovan and my mother do pills, drink and argue about where I was going to sleep. There were no mattresses, so Donovan did the next best thing, he removed two of the televisions from the boxes, crushed the cardboard down and threw it on the floor for me. "Here! You little bad ass boy, sleep on this and if you make a sound or try to run away, I'm going to whoop your little butt!" Donovan said. His mouth was tough, but his private parts were tender. Donovan and my mother cuddled up and fell asleep on their twin size mattress with no sheets, next to the window.

That night, it was very difficult for me to sleep. I was

extremely hungry, cold and I wanted to go home. I finally dozed off and fell into a deep coma-like sleep for a couple of hours, in hopes of waking up from a bad nightmare safe and sound in my comfortable warm bed. Around 7:00 a.m., my eyes popped opened like clockwork. I went over to where Donovan and my mother were sleeping and I pushed her softly to wake her up. I leaned down and whispered in her ear, "Mama, I'm ready to go to school. Mama, I'm ready to go to school." She didn't budge. After a few minutes of pushing and jerking on her, to wake her up, she finally rolled over to me and asked me what I wanted. "Mama, please take me to school. I'm ready to go to school. I can't be late! I can't be late! Mama!" I started yelling frantically. My mother looked at me with a hazy look in her eyes and said, "You're not going to school today." She rolled over and went back to sleep. I lost it! This was the first time I had ever cursed at my mother or any adult for that matter. I shouted, "WHAT THE HELL DO YOU MEAN, I'M NOT GOING TO SCHOOL TODAY? YES, I AM! I'M LEAVING RIGHT NOW!"

My mind and mouth had become more powerful than it had ever been before. I ran back to the other side of the warehouse where I had slept on the cardboard boxes and swooped up my book-bag. I threw on my shoes and raced for the window. I took my bag and threw it out the window then I started to climb after it. Just as I got my left leg and half my body out of the window, I could see and taste the sweet nectar of freedom. My eyes were focused on the fire escape. Suddenly, Donovan grabbed me by the back of my shirt, snatched me back in and threw me on the floor. He started swearing and threatening me again. Only this time, he did it from a distance. I looked over at my mother and she didn't say a word. She just watched him yell at me as if he was my father.

For the next several weeks, Donovan and my mother kept

me hostage in their den of evil and didn't allow me to go to school or even go outside for fresh air. During my stay at the love shack, my diet consisted of sardines, peanut butter, potted meat in the can and potato chips. By this time, my father, grandmother and the entire block was worried. No one had any idea where I was but everyone knew that once they found Donovan, my mother wouldn't be far behind. The word spread through my neighborhood like wildfire that I was missing and was probably with my mother. On an anonymous tip to the police I know came from my guardian angel, the police were lead to investigate the burglary that took place at Fretter's Appliance store.

On the sixteenth day of my kidnapping, my prayers were answered. In the middle of the night, the sound of sirens and thousands of footsteps filled the air. A swarm of angels dressed in police uniforms stormed the warehouse with their weapons drawn to do battle. They found Donovan and my mother passed out on the floor from a full night of partying. As they continued their search, they found me shivering and curled up in the corner. The officer looked down at me, took off his coat, placed it around me and picked me up into his arms. After the handcuffs were slapped on Donovan, the police questioned my mother for several minutes. She boohooed and dropped a few tears, convincing them that Donovan was holding us against our will. They believed her story and released me back to her. As soon as I overheard an officer telling another officer that everything was all right, I could go back with my mother, I jumped out of his arms and yelled, "I WANT TO GO HOME! I WANT TO GO HOME! I WANT TO GO HOME! I'M NOT GOING WITH HER. PLEASE, DON'T MAKE ME GO WITH HER!"

The officer was shocked and just stared at me. I know he was wondering, what could make a little boy not want to go with his mother. He took a step towards me and asked me the Million-dollar question that every police officer asks children that are lost. He said, "Son, do you know your address?" In one elongated breath, I recited all of my information in less than ten seconds.

"Yes sir, I live at 2925 Lycaste, my phone number is 822-0643, my father's name is Larry, my grandmother's name is Granny, I'm eight-years-old, I'm in the third grade, and my teacher's name is Ms. Thomas, I go to Tendler Elementary School, I'm on the honor-roll, I'm never late or tardy, my name is Jonathan Horner, my nickname is John-John and my favorite color is blue and I'm the Master of the Ghetto."

Needless to say, I convinced the officer to take me home. For those two and a half weeks that my mother and Donovan had kidnapped me, I was never afraid because I knew GOD was with me the entire time. Donovan was eventually charged with Grand Theft Larceny and sentenced to three to five years in prison for violating his probation. My mother was released and let off with a warning. The only stipulation for her was that she had to check herself into a rehabilitation center within thirty days after her arrest.

Even though Donovan's physical body was incarcerated, his evil spirit of drug addiction and alcohol abuse lived in my mother for years to come. It took many years of prayer from family and friends along with lots of rehabilitation programs and substance abuse counseling for my mother to completely become clean and free from the devil's grip, which Donovan had placed on her life.

ALL THE GLORY AND POWER BE TO GOD

I am proud to say that my mother is now living a happy, healthy and abundant life, free of alcohol and drugs. Her newfound sobriety landed her into one of the most difficult nursing programs in the country and she graduated at the top of her class. Currently, she is a full-fledged practicing RN at one of the busiest hospitals in Detroit. She also tutors second year nursing students in biology, calculus and advanced science, while taking care of two wonderful children that she adopted.

I love my mother very much and I'm overjoyed that she is doing well. Our relationship at this point in my life is much better. Coincidentally, she lives a mere 15 minutes walking distance from me now. Although our schedules are very hectic, I try to visit her at least once every two weeks to check on her and spend time with her. I also call her when I'm on the road traveling, just to let her know that her little John-John is safe.

What would happen if you were scared half to death twice?

After the traumatizing events of my adolescent years were over and I reached the fifth grade, life was a "piece of cake." The only major ripple was that my dad thought it might be a good idea to change my last name from Horner to Edison to give me a fresh start. I was doing well in school and my life was stable. I was heavily into sports and my grandmother was forcing me to go to church. It seemed that everyone was doing better. Things were going great! My dad had moved on with his life in several different ways. First, he got his love life in order and began dating our next-door neighbor, Ms. Parker's daughter, Sandra. My father was smitten with her from the very beginning. In fact, they were married a few years later. To this day, they are still married with two beautiful children, Sheila, 21, and Dontae, 12.

Second, my dad was also able to find a more stable job that paid him enough money that he no longer had to work a second job. His new position was with the Detroit Water Board Company. Although the money was great, the drawback was that it required him to work outdoors in the elements. He expended twice the physical energy that it required to work both of his old jobs. His hours were shorter, but his workload was more grueling. He would go to work at 7:30 a.m. and get off at 4:30 p.m., but once he got home, he would sleep straight through dinner to almost 10:00 p.m. every night. He called it his beauty rest even though he was grouchy when he got up to eat.

This wasn't a problem for me because my routine after school was simple and precise. Everyday after dismissal, I would run home and make a bologna and cheese sandwich. I quickly changed my clothes, grabbed my basketball, football, bike, and headed down the stairs out the front door. The sport of choice for the afternoon was dependent upon what was going on in my neighborhood. Sometimes, I would take my basketball to the alley across the street from my house and shoot hoops for hours with my best friends, Otis and Donnie. They were cousins. If I were feeling dare-devilish, I would just ride my bike up and down the street popping as many wheelies as I could.

On a hot Thursday afternoon in May, I sat in my classroom waiting for the bell to ring. As soon as we were dismissed, I stayed to my schedule. I ran home, made my bologna and cheese sandwich, then changed my clothes and headed down the stairs with my equipment. I stood on my porch and checked the forecast for the activity that afternoon. I glanced down the street to my left and noticed Otis and Donnie with some of my other friends playing an intense game of tag. I immediately threw my things back inside and ran down the street to join the game. After I arrived on the scene, we all decided to huddle up and start a new game. It was Donnie, Otis, Ki-Ki, Kawana, Nikka and myself. Nikka was it.

Now it was time for the ultimate tag battlefield. Because our parents repeatedly told us not to play in the street, we were forced to play in the vacant lot next door to Ms. Turner's house, Donnie's grandmother. Ms. Turner was a nice lady. She always made us cookies and gave us soft drinks in the summer. Oddly though, she had an infatuation with big German shepherd dogs. As a matter of fact, she had five of them chained in her backyard to keep intruders out. The best thing about Ms. Turner's vacant lot was there was an old 1970 Ford Zephyr sitting in the middle of the lot stripped down and left for dead. Besides the dogs barking at us through the fence, we had a great time.

We played and played until the sun went down. Around 8:00 p.m. that night, we decided to roll out the hose from the side of the house to take a water break. The girls sat on the car. One by one, they drank from the hose. The boys grabbed the hose and, of course, we began wetting all of the girls with it. Before we realized what was going on, we had managed to create a mud moat around the beat up old car. Donnie rolled up the hose and we began to play as we were before. This time, I was it. I closed my eyes, counted to ten and began to give chase around the car as fast as I could. It was difficult for me to keep traction because the Pro-Keds I received from the Good Fellas Charity didn't have any rubber on the bottom of them. I slipped and sloshed through the mud. After several minutes of running, I became exhausted and called a time out.

Approximately five minutes elapsed when I caught my breath and called time in. I started chasing everyone around the car again. We ran around the car to what seemed like hundreds of times laughing and screaming in the joy of childhood, when all of a sudden, everyone in front of me jumped on top of the car. I stopped my chase and yelled, "No fair! You can't jump on the car!" Then the girls started screaming and yelling, "LOOK OUT, JOHN! RUN JOHN! RUN, HE'S RIGHT BEHIND YOU!" My first reaction was to run, but from who? I'm it, until I heard the loudest bark from a dog that I had ever heard in my life. One of Ms. Turner's German Shepherds had gnawed through his chain and jumped over the fence to come after us.

Once I realized that I was about to be eaten alive, I shifted into high gear and tried to outrun the dog using my tag techniques of circling the car. I began the escape from death with a sizable lead, but the dog closed in fast. My heart was pumping through my chest and I couldn't take in any air as he chased me around the car. I was screaming and hollering for my life. About the fifth trip around, my legs got tired and my shoes came off my feet. I tried to jump up on the hood of the car but I wasn't fast enough. The German shepherd took one gigantic leap and dug his claws in my back and snatched me back down into the mud. He started biting and scratching my back and tossing me around like a rag doll. While the dog dragged me back and forth through the mud, the only thing I could do was scream and try to kick him off me.

Meanwhile, all of my friends were paralyzed with fear, standing on top of the car screaming their lungs out, watching the dog maul me. He bit and scratched me so much that I couldn't feel the pain anymore. Then he threw me out of his mouth, head first into the car. As he came back for more, I started kicking the dog repeatedly in the face to try and keep him off of me. It almost worked until he turned his head and bit down on my left leg with the Jaws of Death. That German shepherd began to rip my leg to shreds as I screamed and howled for help. Good thing for me, another angel from God, Donnie's uncle, Kenny, heard me screaming and beat the dog off of me with a black Louisville Slugger baseball bat. My entire body was completely covered in blood, dog saliva and mud. There was blood coming from my head, back, face, neck and leg. Everyone was screaming and I could barely see or hear anything. I was conscious, but everything was moving in slow motion. The girls jumped down off the car and raced up the block to my house to alert my dad and grandmother to what had just happened. They were screaming and yelling so loud that they woke my father out of hibernation.

"MR. EDISON! MR. EDISON, COME QUICK! COME QUICK! JOHN-JOHN IS HURT, HE NEEDS YOUR HELP!" they screamed, yelling up my hallway stairs to my father.

My dad replied, "Well tell him I said to get his butt home right now!"

The girls were stunned. They didn't understand how tough and manly my dad was and how strong he raised me to be.

"NO, MR. EDISON, YOU HAVE TO COME NOW! HE IS

REALLY HURT! THE DOG BIT HIM REALLY BAD! HE'S BLEEDING AND EVERYTHING!"

My dad realized it was serious and I wasn't able to walk home. He quickly threw on his clothes and ran down the street to rescue me.

That single dog attack caused me to receive two skin graphs, 160 stitches and physical therapy treatments on my left leg for the next three years.

Thank you, Kenny Bell, for saving my life.

As I grew older and became more independent, my dad started to place more responsibility on me. In the middle of my sixth grade year, my father sat me down and told me I was going to have to start thinking more maturely as I entered into my manhood. At 11-years-old, what did I know about thinking more maturely? I had just stopped wetting the bed and wearing superhero pajamas. He explained to me that all responsible men knew how to take care of themselves. What did this mean? I could barely pee straight, let alone take care of myself. I had no clue to what he was talking about.

The next week, the lessons began: Cooking and Cleaning 101. Early one Saturday morning at the crack of dawn, my dad woke me up out of a sound sleep. He handed me a bucket, a mop, a broom, a dust pan, a can of Ajax, a bottle of Pine Sol, three rags and a three-pack of yellow latex gloves and said, "Let's hit it!" As I slowly made my way out of bed, I thought to myself, "This dude is going crazy!" That morning I must have wiped, cleaned, scoured and mopped everything in the house that had a surface on it. By 11:00 a.m., I was completely exhausted. My hands were beginning to turn pale from constantly dunking them in the buckets of hot, soapy water. At 2:00 p.m. that afternoon, I was finally released from duty. I could barely wait to peel the soaked latex gloves off my hands and the clothes that stuck to my body like glue from all the sweat and dirty water. Later my dad came into my room and asked me if I had learned anything that day. Little did he know that he was about to get the same thing I had given Donovan, for working my fingers to the bone. Fortunately for him, I was feeling merciful that day and I just nodded my head and replied, "Yes sir. I learned a lot." That afternoon, I climbed in bed and slept right through dinner and into the next day. I didn't wake up until it was time for me to go to church the next morning.

After church that afternoon, I came home to find my father waiting in the kitchen for me with an apron, a towel, a potato peeler and a 50 lb. bag of Idaho white potatoes. One by one, I peeled and peeled and peeled those potatoes for hours. The entire time, my dad remained completely silent. He just stood over me and watched to see if I would finish the bag. When I got down to the bottom of the bag, my hands began to cramp. My eyes started tearing up because I was so upset at him for making me peel all those damn potatoes. When I finished peeling the last three, I turned around to see the look on his face, but he was gone. I dropped the potato peeler and ran out of the kitchen to find him. A few seconds later, I found him lying in bed watching television with his feet propped up. I was furious as I stood at the door in total disgust. Before I could say anything, he turned to me and said, "Good job, son. Now go and get cleaned up." After several weeks of Basic Training 101, I quickly moved from peeling potatoes to baking homemade rolls.

By the time I was in the seventh grade, I could cook, clean and keep a house better than the average woman. I later figured out that my dad's mission was to groom me to be a complete and self-sufficient young man with character and values. He had achieved his goal. By the summer of that year,

I had completely taken over the house and my main focus was taking care of my grandmother. Although she was well enough at that time to move around, her health was beginning to diminish. I cooked all her meals, helped her around the house, ran her errands and still managed to play little league basketball three days per week.

At this point in my life, my granny was everything to me. She was the most incredible woman I knew in the world. She was strong, tough, straightforward, and could hold her own with the best of them. Most importantly, she loved me unconditionally. Even though she wasn't my birth mother, she took care of me as if I was her only son. And, regardless of the mistakes I made, she never criticized me or beat me down verbally. She may have popped me upside the head with her cane every now and then, but we were inseparable. Granny was the glue and the foundation that held us together as a family unit.

No matter what went on in my life, she was always there for me. My first bout with the chickenpox, she was there. The night my temperature shot up to 103 degrees, she was there. The day neighborhood bullies jumped on me after school, she was there. The nights I had nightmares about my mother and couldn't get back to sleep, she was there. When I accidentally set my dad's bed on fire, she was there. The Sunday I ran out of church in fear because a woman next to me caught the Holy Ghost, she was there. When I decided I was grown and challenged my father to a fistfight, she was there, THANK GOD! I can't say enough about my granny. I loved her with every ounce of my soul.

My eighth-grade year of school started off with a bang. The Chrysler Corporation notified us that they were buying the property in our area and converting it into a Chrysler Jeep Plant. This was good news for us, because it meant that they were going to pay off our old house and relocate us into a brand new home. A few weeks later, I was hit with the best news of my life. I received a letter of acceptance to Cass Technical High School, one of the premier high schools in Detroit. My grandmother and father were so proud of me because their boy was going to Cass Tech. My granny was especially proud of me. She couldn't believe that her little grandson was on his way to high school.

In May we moved into our new home, which was located in a different area of Detroit's eastside. The house was beautiful and the neighborhood was very peaceful. That summer was a time of love for my dad. He decided to keep a room at our house but, ultimately, he moved in with his new wife into their new apartment. My life was perfect again. I had a new home, a new set of friends and I was on my way to Cass Technical High School. I even found a summer job at Bob & Don's Meat Market around the corner from my house. I worked a couple of days per week, played basketball until the sun went down, and took care of my grandmother. The only difference in my life was that I was more focused on perfecting my basketball game in hopes of one day living my dream of playing professionally.

The summer, that year, was extremely hot. Unfortunately, our house was not equipped with air conditioning. This was a problem for my grandmother because her health wasn't the greatest at the time. She'd recently had a mild stoke on her left side. In addition, she suffered from shortness of breath and hot flashes. Yet, we made do with what we had. I managed to rig a fan in her bedroom window to help keep her cool. As usual, before I left the house to practice my game, I would check on my grandmother to see if she was hungry or if she needed anything. If she did, I served it to her and headed for the basketball court. Usually, I provided her with a glass of water, her medicine, some food and a cold towel for her head.

On this particular day in August, the temperature had reached well over 100 degrees. I decided to sleep in and give the heat a chance to cool down. When I went in to check on my grandmother that afternoon at 12:30 p.m., she didn't look so good but she said she felt fine and all she needed was a piece of fruit and a glass of water. I took the pitcher of water out of the refrigerator and grabbed a peach for her to eat. I returned to her room and set the glass of water on her nightstand and placed the peach in her hand with the same love and care she had always given me. Then I went back to my room and laid across my bed under the ceiling fan. At 6:00 p.m., after watching all of the television I could tolerate, I threw my basketball shorts on and headed down the hall to look in on her once again before leaving the house. I peeked my head in the door.

I said, "Hey, granny! Do you want something to eat right now or do you want to wait until I get back?"

Honestly, I was hoping she would say that she could wait until I got back, because I couldn't stand being cooped up in the house one more second. In a light somber voice, she said, "Yes son. Make your granny something to eat right now before you go."

"Okay, granny. What do you feel like having today?" I asked. She looked up at me, smiled and said, "Granny's kind of hungry today. I feel like I want meatballs smothered in gravy, white rice, cabbage, black-eyed peas, cornbread muffins and walnut brownies for dessert." My mouth hit the floor. I couldn't believe she had requested so much food. I asked, "Are you sure, granny? That seems like a lot of food."

She just smiled back at me and nodded as if to say she knew. Nevertheless, I went to the kitchen to get dinner started for her. In the midst of my cooking, there was a knock at my side door. It was three of my new buddies who lived down the street. They were basketball fanatics like myself. I opened the door, slapped a few hands together and told them I would meet them at the court in a few minutes, but first I had to finish cooking my grandmother's dinner. They laughed and laughed.

"John you're crazy. You know you don't know how to cook. You're just scared to come out because you know it's over for you once you step on the court."

I just smiled at them and then tried to defend myself verbally, but it didn't work. So I decided to give them a taste of the Master Chef's work. I reached in the oven, pulled out the smothered meatballs simmering in gravy, then took a fork, split one down the middle and gave it to them. "Man! This is good! John, you really can cook," they said.

"Yeah, I know. Now get out!" I replied.

After I threw them out, I finished off my grandmother's meal by making her a fresh glass of brisk iced tea, her favorite. When the entire meal was completely finished, I prepared her plate and carried it to her room. I sat the food on the dresser, reached underneath the bed to get her food tray and got her all set up. While I helped her with her napkin, she looked up at me with her beautiful brown eyes and said, "You're such a good grandson. Come and give an old lady a kiss." I kissed my granny on her forehead, ran to my room and threw on my shoes. Then I grabbed my basketball and headed for the court.

On my way down the driveway, I suddenly remembered that I had forgotten to give her the iced tea I had made for her. I ran back up the driveway to the side door, which led to the kitchen and grabbed the tea out of the refrigerator. As I carried the tea to her room, I was anxious to see the look on her face of her enjoying the meal. But what I saw after I entered the room was the most horrifying scene I had ever witnessed in my life. My grandmother was lying on the floor face down and unresponsive. I dropped the glass of tea I was holding in my hand and starting crying deliriously.

For the next few minutes, my body experienced a form of petrifaction that seemed to suspend time with everything around me. Once the grief and pain that came over me released my body to react, panic began to set in. I began to breath very deeply and tears poured out of my eyes as if my body was flooding on the inside. Once I regained as much composure as I could, I quickly ran across the street to a neighbor's house to get help. I fought through tears, pain and fear to explain to Mrs. Elliot what was going on. She dialed 911 immediately, then I gave her the number for my father and she called him too. After the calls were made, we both ran to my house and hurried to my grandmother's side. We were afraid to move her so Mrs. Elliot tried talking to her, but didn't get a response. A few minutes later, the ambulance and my dad arrived almost simultaneously. They rushed straight to my grandmother. While everyone scrambled to find her medication and gather up her belongings, the para-medics had put her on the gurney and began to wheel my granny to the ambulance. My dad and I jumped in his car and followed close behind the ambulance to the hospital.

Before we made it to the hospital, I had already prayed to GOD several times for Him to make my grandmother better again. I asked Him to save her and to restore her strength, so she could return home safely.

I prayed, "GOD, my granny needs your help. She's not doing very well and I need you to help her."

That's what they taught us in the church she forced me to go to, "If you pray to GOD and asked for His help, He would help you, because GOD loves everyone." At the hospital, my dad and I rushed into the waiting room looking for a doctor or nurse to speak with. As hard as I tried to hold back my tears, the soul-shattering image of my grandmother lying on her bedroom floor overpowered my body. Suddenly, in the middle of the waiting room, I began screaming and crying as if someone were beating me to death. My dad rushed over to me, put his arms around me and said, "Everything is going to be okay. She's going to be fine, I guarantee you!" I nodded my head and my body felt numb as we sat in the waiting room lobby, waiting for the doctor to return.

After three hours of waiting, the doctor my dad talked with when we first arrived at the hospital came out to give us an update on my grandmother's condition. I watched my dad walk through the double glass doors and I began to pray again, "GOD, I'm begging you, please make my grandmother well again. Please make her well again!" I tried to read the doctors lips as he explained to my dad about my grandmother's status, but he was talking too fast. My dad and the doctor were just nodding back and forth as they looked at charts. My worst fear became a reality when I saw the doctor put his hand on my father's shoulder to ease the blow. When my dad's head dropped, I knew she was dead. At that very moment, while sitting right in the hospital, I cursed GOD, my church and my overdressed pastor. I vowed never to pray or step foot into another church again as long as I lived. That night, as I sat on the edge of my bed motionless, I tried to imagine what life was going to be like with the center of my life gone.

After a long sleepless night, my dad came into my room the next morning. He sat down and talked to me for a long time about how life goes on after death. He tried to explain to me that my granny was in a better place. He did a pretty good job of it, but I wasn't paying attention. I could see his lips moving as he talked to me, but there was no sound coming out. The only sound I could hear was my grandmother's voice playing in my head over and over and over. That night before I closed my eyes to go to sleep, I pictured my granny flying over the city on a beautiful white cloud. She was wearing her best Sunday dress and she was absolutely beautiful.

CHAPTER TWO

*A Golden Opportunity To
Give Up!
(The Man)*

The Good, The Bad And The Ugly

After my grandmother's death, life for me was never the same. I stopped going to church and I developed a callous heart towards everything. My dad suggested that I come live with him but I refused. I knew they only had a two-bedroom apartment and I wasn't about to leave my home to go sleep in a room with my younger sister, Sheila. And besides, I wanted to be as close to my grandmother in memory as I could, even though she was gone. So my father and I agreed that I could continue to live in the house as long as I wanted if I attended school and continued to work. The arrangement was perfect for me because I was able to maintain my freedom and live in the place that I considered to be home.

After a couple of weeks of working and going to school, I began to enjoy the idea of taking care of myself. Not only was I king of my domain, but I was also able to carry the responsibilities of an adult. I didn't have anyone to answer to and my time was free for me to spend however I pleased. At age 13, I was the world's youngest working, most eligible bachelor. As the months passed, my dad came by the house almost every day to check on things. He was actually surprised and relieved that I hadn't burned the house down or destroyed any of the contents with my new Hulk Hogan wrestling moves. On most afternoons he would come by, we would sit and talk for hours and hours about life and the importance of being a good citizen. He would call it our time to have a family meeting or a father and son bonding session. I would call it the NEW WORLD ORDER, NON-DENOMINATIONAL PREACHING: FEATURING PASTOR, DOCTOR, PHILOSOPHER AND TEACHER WITH MR. LARRY EDISON.

My pops would talk and talk and talk until I felt like snatching my ears off my head. He reminded me of a motor with a three-hour string attached to it and somebody had reached behind his head and pulled it. After several weeks of lectures and dissertations given by my father, he decided that it would be profitable for us if I had a roommate in the house. He told me that he was a little worried about me living in the house by myself and he would feel a little safer if someone was there with me to watch the house when I wasn't home. I bought into the idea but I knew it was more about the bucks than my safety. My dad was an entrepreneur by nature and he felt that he should take advantage of every opportunity.

That Saturday, a few days after our conversation, he came over to the house and told me that he had a coworker by the name of Carrie who had a son that was in his early thirties who was looking for, and needed a place to live. I didn't think anything of it. My first thought was it might be kind of cool to have another man in the house. Especially someone closer to my own age that could relate to some of the things I was going through as a teenager. Later that evening, Eddie, my soon-to-be roommate, wanted to come by to check out the house and his room. He seemed to be pretty cool and he liked sports, but he wore bifocals that looked like huge pop bottles. They made him look like a nerd. After we talked for a few minutes, I showed him around the place. He was quite impressed with the layout and asked me if I thought it was all right for him to move in. Without any concern, I said, "Sure, why not?" He seemed to be a nice guy and my dad was a friend of his mother.

The very next day, my dad, Eddie and I sat down in the living room and talked about the rules and regulations of the house. For me, things were pretty much the same. I was free to come and go as I pleased, but I had to respect the fact that my new roommate was older than me. For Eddie, the rules my dad laid out were simple. He told him that he should be mindful and respect the fact that I was still in high school and I was still very young and impressionable. He also informed him that having parties all night and bringing three and four women in the house was definitely a no-no and a cause for immediate eviction. Before my dad turned over the keys, Eddie swore that he would stick to the rules and was definitely not going to have any women in the house partying or otherwise. My dad and Eddie shook hands and Eddie moved in the following Saturday.

In the beginning, it was a little awkward having Eddie move in because he moved into my grandmother's old room. I held that room in the house sacred. After the initial shock wore off, I soon accepted the fact that I needed to move on and allow my grandmother's soul to rest in peace. In November, everything was flowing like clockwork. Eddie and I were both gone all day, neither one of us did much cooking. Most nights he would spring for pizza or McDonald's. On the weekends, he would stay home and have his best friend from college, Trevor, come over. Trevor was a pretty cool guy as well. He always bragged about how many women he had and how easy it was for him to get a date. After a few weekends, I noticed that Eddie never had any women over to the house. But then I remembered my father's voice. I could hear him saying, "Don't have women in the house partying."

It was a cold Saturday night in January, when I was introduced to a part of life that I had only heard about. That afternoon, Eddie walked into my bedroom and asked me about my plans for the evening. I told him, "I don't have any plans. I'm just going to hang out at the house because my funds are low." I had spent my last $130 on a new pair of Jordan's that had just hit the shelves. He laughed and said, "Man you should get out of here tonight. Teenagers shouldn't be stuck in the house on a Saturday night." That was funny because I was thinking the same thing. Then he reached in his pocket and pulled out a $100 bill and told me to call a couple of my buddies and treat them to the movies and dinner. I couldn't believe my ears. I was experiencing every teenager's dream, a free night out with my buddies. I snatched the hundred out of his hand quicker than Muhammad Ali throws a punch. I called up a couple of my friends. We met at my house and left from there to the movies.

After a full night of movies, junk food and hamburgers, I was ready to go home, kick my shoes off and sleep until the sun came up. As I approached the house, I noticed Trevor's car in the driveway. I started laughing to myself because I knew exactly what they were doing. That's right — girls, girls, girls, partying in the house. Not wanting to interrupt, I tiptoed around to the back of the house and entered through the den door. As soon as I opened the door I heard Teddy Pendergrass "Turn Off The Lights" blasting throughout the house. As I walked in the kitchen, I heard a provocative sound of moaning in the background.

A voice screaming, *"Oh Trevor! Oh Trevor! Give it to me, daddy! Oh Trevor, don't stop, don't stop, don't stop!"*

Then I heard Trevor, *"That's right baby! Who's your daddy? Who's your daddy? Oooooh yeah, keep it right there baby!"*

I burst out laughing! I couldn't believe it! Trevor wasn't lying, he really was the man! Curiosity took control of my feet and my body and I was forced to investigate. Quietly, I

49

slipped into the hall like the Pink Panther. Then I heard it again. "Oh Trevor. Do it, daddy! Do it, daddy! Yeah baby! Yeah baby! Give it to me, baby! Give it to me, baby!" I started laughing so hard in the hallway that I almost urinated on myself. This woman sounded like she was having a ball, no pun intended. I finally pulled myself together and crept to the bedroom door. It was cracked opened and I peeked inside. As soon as I saw her I started screaming, "OH MY GOD! OH MY GOD! OH MY GOD!" It was Eddie, wearing a blonde wig, butt-naked, on his knees. His lips were painted candy apple red, and he was wearing a pair of red high heel pumps with two black garter belts on both of his thighs. Trevor was dripping with sweat, strapped on the back of Eddie, humping and pumping away like a jackrabbit in heat. They were so engaged in each other that they didn't even hear me yelling, or see me standing in the doorway. Then as they went to change positions, I ran down into the basement and tried to digest what I had just witnessed. But before I knew it, I was standing over the basement sink vomiting violently because my nerves were going haywire.

Twenty minutes later, I guess they were finished. I heard footsteps walking overhead and suddenly the music stopped. Then the pipes in the basement started screaming from someone turning on the shower in the bathroom. This was a good opportunity for me to sneak out of the house and come in through the side door as though I were arriving home for the first time. I was in such shock, I didn't want to believe what I had just seen. In deep thought, I took my key and opened the door. I headed straight for my bedroom. As I traveled through the kitchen, I noticed Eddie standing alone looking in the refrigerator, completely back to normal. He was wigless, and in men's house shoes and wearing his thick glasses again. He had pulled a real life *Clark Kent/Lois Lane* act on me. As I walked by him, my entire body started to

50

tremble and I couldn't catch my breath. I didn't say anything to him. I just walked right past him into my room and closed the door. How in hell could I explain what I had just witnessed to my father? He was the manliest man that I knew. To put it simply, if the government started arresting men who had an ounce of weakness or female tendencies within them, my father would be a FREE MAN.

My dad despised homosexuality. He told me when I was younger that if I ever brought a boyfriend home, he would kill us both and anybody that looked like him. I knew if I told my father what had happened, there was going to be hell to pay. So I decided that the best thing to do was keep it to myself. I kept it bottled up deep inside me because I didn't want to deal with it, until the day their relationship got out of control. For the next three months, the charade continued. I pretended that I didn't know what was happening and Eddie pretended that Trevor was just his best friend. It was so strange watching them hide their relationship. Trevor was starting to stay over several days during the week. They made excuses that his car was not operating properly, or he was too tired to make the drive. He would start out sleeping on the couch and end up in the bed with Eddie in the middle of the night.

One night, after a long day of school and basketball practice, I came home and jumped right into bed and fell into a deep, hibernating type sleep. Around 1:30 a.m. in the morning, while I was dreaming of my days in the NBA, I rolled over and felt something strange and warm on the back of my leg, but I didn't wake up completely. A few seconds later, there it was again, moving up and down my leg. I rolled over to see what it was and I nearly lost my mind! It was freshly squeezed semen running down my leg. Trevor had come into my room in the middle of the night and masturbated over me while I slept. Once I woke up completely, he was still standing there, butt-naked, basking in the after glow with a bottle of Johnson's Baby Oil in his right hand.

In that moment, I wanted to beat him half to death. With his eyes still closed, I punched him right in his nose. I could hear it break on contact. As he tried to escape the butt whooping, I punched him in the back of his head and he went flying into the mirror on my dresser. The mirror shattered and cut his hands, face and feet really bad. Then I reached over to my weight bench and grabbed a 20 lb. dumbbell to hit him over the head with it. The next thing I knew, Eddie came running into my bedroom screaming, "Stop! Please, John, you're killing him! Stop! John, please stop! He's not breathing!" He was right, I realized I was about to kill him and I stopped. While Trevor lay on my bedroom floor bleeding like a stuck pig, I started yelling, "YOU FAG! YOU FAG! YOU PUNK! YOU PUNK! IF YOU EVER TOUCH ME AGAIN, I'M GOING TO KILL YOU!" I tried to calm down, but I couldn't. I was furious. I ran down to the basement and got my bat to kick his butt some more, but when I returned, they were gone. Once I realized that they were gone, I went back to my bedroom. I sat on my weight bench and began to cry. I felt violated, ashamed and guilty for not waking up in time to stop him. That night, I stood by the door in tears with my bat waiting for them to come back but they never showed up.

My dad came over the next day to find out what had happened. Eddie had called him that morning, saying I was a maniac out of control and he didn't know why. My dad came over and immediately he noticed the dried blood in the carpet, the broken mirror, and the bloody handprints on my dresser and door. Then he sat down, looked me in my eyes and asked, "BOY, WHAT THE HELL HAPPENED HERE? BOY, CAN YOU HEAR ME? JOHN! JOHN! JOHN! JOHN! CAN YOU HEAR ME?"

I didn't respond. I just sat there staring at him with a blank expression on my face. Psychologically, I was traumatized and I never told my dad exactly what happened but we agreed that Eddie had to go.

What Do You Mean I'm Kicked Out?

With the trauma of my grandmother's death fresh on my mind, intimidating talk about high school from my middle school teachers, and the lack of social readiness, I entered into one of the most academically challenging and largest high schools in my city with FEAR strapped to me like a helmet. I went from a middle school with three levels, a student body of 600, roughly 35 teachers, one gym, a swimming pool that only worked half the time, and a small cafeteria, to a school with eight levels, a student body of 2,000, well over 150 teachers, three gyms and a cafeteria the size of a convention center.

I was so overwhelmed by the girth of the school and the shear madness that took place every day that I decided not to attend class. Instead, I hung out with the upper classmen who were professional skippers. It was like clockwork every day from 8:00 a.m. to 12:35 p.m. We would hang out at the store that was a block and half away from the school. This went on for about four weeks. When I did decide to attend class, it wasn't because I wanted to get an education. It was because all of the classes were packed with beautiful young girls who needed a "BIG DADDY" in their life.

For the entire first semester of school, I was lost, confused and I had developed a poor self-image. The amount of pressure to do well and fit in was too much for me, not to mention that I had all of this other drama going on in my life. I had six classes including basketball practice and chores at home, plus I worked 30 hours per week. No class in middle school had prepared me for this tremendous transition. I felt like a little paddleboat being tossed to and fro in the ocean of peer pressure, emotional baggage and chaos. I was not able to focus and, more importantly, I didn't have anyone to go to for help. I depended on the guys that I skipped school with to guide and lead me.

At the conclusion of the first semester, my counselor, who I had never met before, called me down to her office to give me an academic warning letter. She told me, "Jonathan, it has come to our attention that your grades are very poor at this point. You received a 1.7 and a 1.5 on your first two report cards and that's not acceptable. Cass Tech is a high academic school of choice and if your grades don't improve, you may suffer the consequences of being asked to leave. Therefore, from this point on, Mr. Edison, you will be placed on academic probation."

I left her office with my heart in my stomach. I had never been on academic probation or any type of probation for that matter. I considered myself to be a smart kid. How could I be doing so terrible now? The thought of me being on academic probation did even more damage to my self-esteem and fanned the flame of my poor self-image. At this point, I became more focused on trying to fit in and hide the fact that I was on academic probation and my grades became even worse.

After the third card marking, my confidence, self esteem and hunger for knowledge had evaporated. I received my report card and it was a whopping 1.4. The peer pressure, my home life, and expectation of being an adult trapped inside a 13-year-old's body was too much for me to manage. Because I used my grade point average as a barometer to measure how smart I was and who I was according to the standards set by society, I started to believe that I was a dumb, good-for-nothing kid, who didn't deserve the right to attend Cass Technical High School. By the time the second semester rolled around, it was time for me to face the music.

At 9:00 a.m. on a Friday morning, my principal announced over the intercom the names of 30 students with instructions to report to the office to receive a letter to take home. I sat in French class, clutching my desk, hoping he wouldn't call my name. "Larry Alexander, Jenny Bee, Lawrence Carte, Clyde Donald, Mary Eason, JONATHAN EDISON," he announced. I almost fainted right there in class. What could this mean? What does he want? Why is he calling me? Five hundred other questions ran through my mind. My teacher looked at me and gave me the nod to go, so I excused myself and began my journey to the office. As I walked down the eight flights of stairs, I tried to imagine that I was back in my old neighborhood carrying my bike down the stairs and getting ready to pop wheelies. I was soon snapped back to reality by the buzz of 30 other ninth graders that I ran into on our walk to the main office. No one knew for sure why we had been summoned, but everyone had his or her own idea. Speculations ran rapid.

"What's this about? I know! Somebody was fighting. No! A girl was cheating on a test and they think we know something about it. No! No! I know, we all might be receiving a special reward or something." It had to be something serious. We all waited outside the office for the secretary to call our names one by one. Once she got to my name, I went into the office and she handed me a manila envelope that contained the death of my spirit, enthusiasm, and love for school, education and myself. The letter read:

> *To the parents of Jonathan Edison,*
> *Due to poor academic performance and low achievement, your son/daughter, Jonathan Edison, who's current grade point average is a 1.59, may not, cannot and will not be allowed to return to Cass Technical High School in the fall of*

1988. It is apparent that the rigors of such a demanding environment is too much for him/her to handle right now. So it is with deep regret that we must inform you that your son/daughter has been academically dismissed. Remember he/she is no longer a Cass Technical High School student and should not return to the school grounds. He/she is to report to his neighborhood high school to continue his/her education.

P.S. His/her report card will be mailed within 5 to 6 weeks. Have a great summer.

I stood outside the main office and read that letter and I wanted to take a gun to my head and blow my brains out. I felt like the biggest failure on the planet. I could not understand how I could transform from a model student who loved school to a kid now kicked out of a school for low academic achievement. As I returned to my class with this letter crumbled up in my hand, I decided to drop out of school.

When The Love Is Gone

At age 14, all of the love in my heart was completely evanescent. My love for life, my love for school, my love for GOD and my love for myself. My mind was in such mental turmoil that I became heedless and hazardous to myself. I began to stay out all times of night walking the streets and wondering what life was going to throw at me next. With the burden of being kicked out of school on my mind and the secret of Eddie and Trevor seared into my psyche, my peace of mind was now my worst enemy. As I looked for someone to empathize my plight, I turned to a buddy of mine.

He lived on the same block and was already a high school dropout. His name was Jerome Bailey. Jerome was 16-years-old and stood 6'8" inches tall. He lived a few doors down from me and he had dropped out of high school because his basketball coach didn't select him for the basketball team during his ninth grade year. He was so devastated that he gave up going to school and stayed home everyday drowning his sorrows in malt liquor and marijuana. He was the perfect role model I needed to help me with my problem. I found myself sitting in his living room watching him smoke marijuana and drink beer. Then after a few sips of Old English Malt Liquor and a couple of whiffs of second hand marijuana smoke, I was hooked. Oddly though, the only thing that interrupted my process of enjoyment was myself. Beer and weed made me violently ill immediately afterwards. I tried to do it but my body wouldn't allow me. Thank God.

In late July, my dad sold our house. He managed to secure a three-bedroom apartment, which provided enough room for me to have my own bedroom. We packed all of my things and I moved in with my new family. It was instantaneous hostility created by the move. Things were different because I was accustomed to coming and going as I pleased, cooking what I wanted and when I wanted. In my mind, I was a grown man and deserved to be treated like one. But my stepmother didn't see it that way. She wanted me to follow her rules and her rules only. That meant no cooking in the house after 8:00 p.m., no visitors of any kind, no leaving out of the house after 9:00 p.m., no staying up past 11:00 p.m., and definitely no wrestling moves on her couch or in her living room. Her number one rule, which she constantly reminded me of, was to "LET THE TOILET SEAT DOWN AFTER I USED IT!" She was so obsessed with that damn toilet seat rule that she made a sign especially for me. "MAKE SURE YOU PUT THE TOILET SEAT DOWN!!"

"She colored it bright red and taped it on my bedroom door with duct tape. This of course was a problem for me but that wasn't the worst of it.

A couple of weeks went by and I noticed that my father was beginning to take her side on every issue concerning me. He would come home from work and give me a speech regarding her unhappiness, reminding me of how I never put the toilet seat down and how I made her feel bad by disrespecting her rules. He reminded me of every little damn thing I did ... I eat too much, I make too much noise, I take showers too long, I leave the toilet seat up, I slam the door too hard, I don't talk to my sister enough, I can't be trusted, I make her nervous, I talk too much, I laugh too loud. You name it and I did it, according to her. I felt like my father had turned against me. After the third week of living with them, I had enough. I couldn't take it anymore. I made up my mind that it was either her or me, but somebody had to go. I didn't care that she was the woman of the house and she didn't care that I thought that I was grown either.

One night I stayed out until about 12:30 a.m. in the morning. When I returned to the apartment, she was awake waiting for me. As soon as I walked through the door, she started yelling and screaming at me about how stupid I was and how I didn't listen and how she wished I had never been born. The next morning, I told my dad what had happened the night before.

He started yelling, "BOY, DON'T YOU EVER TALK TO MY WIFE LIKE THAT AGAIN AS LONG AS YOU LIVE. ARE YOU STUPID OR SOMETHING? YOU BETTER GET YOUR ACT TOGETHER BEFORE I SEND YOU TO JUVENILE OR SOMETHING!" I was so frustrated that I fired back at him, "YOU KNOW WHAT? THIS IS SOME B.S. BOTH OF YOU ARE CRAZY! YOU KNOW WHAT? I'M SICK OF LIVING HERE ANYWAY! YOU DON'T HAVE TO SEND ME ANYWHERE! I'LL LEAVE ON MY OWN! YOU DON'T WANT ME HERE ANYWAY!"

My father stood back with his fist in gear. He yelled,

"WHEN ARE YOU LEAVING?" I yelled back, "RIGHT NOW!"

Then I ran up to my room, grabbed my book bag, suitcase and my life's savings of $300 that I had in my closet and I ran back down the stairs. I stormed passed my father and left. I didn't know where I was going; I just knew I had to go. I walked and walked and walked for hours, which felt like days. By the time I realized where I was, I had nearly walked all the way to my old high school. That was about 12 miles away from my dad's house. As the sun went down, I found myself in a place called Cass Corridor. As you can probably tell just by the name, Cass Corridor was not a friendly place in the city. Cass Corridor was and still is plagued with drugs, prostitution, homelessness, and sleazy one-hour motels that johns and hookers use for pleasure and entertainment. As I entered into the gates of hell, I had flashbacks of my childhood, walking to the Food Stamp Office with my mother. The only difference now, she wasn't there with me and the streets were lined with hypodermic needles, used sanitary napkins, homeless prostitutes and used condoms filled with unborn babies. All of that didn't matter though. I was tired, hungry, hurt, disgusted and fed up with my father and his wife. I wondered, how could he choose that woman over me? I'm his son. What is he doing? If that's how he wants it, fine. No problem. That's how it's going to be!

I convinced myself that I would be all right and I proceeded on with my journey through Lucifer's love den. I walked up to the counter of one of the one-hour motels and I checked into the vilest place on earth. I paid $18 for the entire night, got my key and headed for the room. When I opened the door, the smell of urine attacked me and knocked me down to my knees. I didn't have any other place to go so I covered my mouth and went in. The room was dark and filthy. This place had a fresh coat of sin and demonic spirits on the walls and the floor. There was no running water and no room service. The bed was a sheetless, twin sized mattress sitting on a cot in the middle of the floor, which contained the history of thousands of unspeakable sex acts. The only good thing was that the lamp worked and it allowed me to keep an eye on the roaches that were trying to climb into my nice warm suitcase. After settling into the Bellagio, my stomach began to growl. I was hungry but I was too tired and afraid to make a trip to the store in fear of being robbed or attacked.

Needless to say, I fell asleep with a huge plate of fried chicken, macaroni and cheese, collard greens, mashed potatoes, candied yams, biscuits and grape Kool-Aid on my mind. The next morning, a loud banging on the door woke me up!

"HEY, BOY! WAKE UP! IT'S TIME TO GO. COME ON, LET'S GO! EITHER PAY NOW FOR ANOTHER NIGHT OR GET OUT! BOY, DO YOU HEAR ME IN THERE? IT'S TIME TO GO!"

I started to gather up all my things then I quickly realized that I had no place to go. I opened the door and paid the guy for a week in advance and planned to stay as long as my money lasted or until an Angel rescued me. On the sixth night, I was on my way to the party store. A woman by the name of Mary, a long time friend of my mother's, saw me walking and stopped me.

"John-John, is that you? John-John, come here, son! What in the world are you doing here in Cass Corridor? Are you crazy? Don't you know what type of neighborhood you're in? Where do you live? Come on, I'll take you there!" she said.

I told her that I lived in the "you pay and you play" one-hour motel a few blocks up the street. Her eyes almost jumped out of her head. Then with tears running down my face, I proceeded to tell her that I had run away from my father's house, my grandmother was dead, and I didn't know where my mother was living. Mary's face became stricken with grief and she began to cry as if someone close in her family had died. Then she told me to get in the car, check out of the Dew Drop Inn, and she would take me to my aunt's house until we could figure everything out. My Aunt Elizabeth was my mother's sister who lived near the Detroit City Airport and she was also a nurse. After 30 minutes of driving, we finally arrived at my aunt's house and, fortunate for me, she was home. Mary explained to her what was going on and she felt sympathetic to my situation and agreed to allow me to live there if I promised to clean up after myself and paid her $50 a month in rent. I agreed.

A few days later, I worked up enough courage to call my father. I made arrangements to pick up the remainder of my things. My cousin Jamall, who had a pick up truck at the time, volunteered to help me go pick up my furniture. But when we arrived, my dad was not in the mood for any games. I rang the bell and he opened the door and asked me what I wanted, like I was a stranger. I told him that I needed my bedroom furniture for my room at my aunt's house. Then he made it very clear that the only thing that belonged to me were the clothes on my back. "You're not taking anything out of this house. You can have the mattress and that's it."

At that moment I felt like punching him right in the mouth, but I didn't. I may have been stupid, but I wasn't crazy. I ran up the stairs, stripped down the bed and hauled the mattress outside to the truck. The entire time my dad never said a word. He just waited for me to clear the threshold of the front door and locked it behind me. There I was, in tears, driving through busy intersections with my cousin and my mattress on my way to unfamiliar territory. I really didn't want to go but pride wouldn't allow me to stay.

Deja Vue/ Could It Get Any Worse?

The condition of my aunt's house was not the greatest, but it was a place to live. I set up camp in the basement near the furnace. I had to put my mattress up on crates because the floor had flooded with mildewed sewer water as a result of bad plumbing. I kept my clothes inside a black plastic garbage bag so they wouldn't smell like mildew. I didn't have a television or radio but the dripping water from the sweating pipes and the hum of the furnace when it kicked on provided me with enough mental Chinese torture chamber music to satisfy my crave of rhythm and beats. For 50 bucks a month this was the equivalent of the Trump Towers to me. I still had my job at Bob & Don's Meat Market but I decided to give them a rest and try the restaurant business. I took a bus to Chili's Grill & Bar, which was about 20 miles away from my aunt's house, and got a job washing dishes and bussing tables earning $5.25 an hour for the dishes and $2.51 an hour for the bussing.

It was mid August and I didn't really know if I wanted to go back to school or not, but my aunt, a strong advocate of education, convinced me to give high school a try. With her persuasion, at the beginning of September, I went and registered at my neighborhood high school, which was Osborn High. The day before registration, some of the students that lived on my block filled my head with horror stories of what went on inside Osborn. They told me about the gangs, the violence, the drugs, the lack of security and the metal detectors that everyone was required to walk through in order to gain entrance to the building. I paused and thought for a moment, if they have all those things going on, it would take the focus off me and how dumb I was. I felt it would be easier to fit in and go unnoticed, rather than try to outshine and make waves with the other students. Once I realized that the kids on my block were not exaggerating in the slightest, it was a total 180-degree turn from what I was accustomed to at my former high school. Kids were fighting in the hallway, kicking over vending machines, openly selling drugs and even beating up teachers.

I couldn't believe the chaos that was going inside the school. I did my best to steer clear of the violence, unruliness and mayhem that took place. Instead, I chose to focus on working and trying to save money to buy another pair of AIR Jordan's, to keep up with the latest fashion. Several years went by and I began to blend in with the crowd so well that no one even noticed me. I wasn't a bad kid, but I wasn't exceptionally bright either. I didn't have all F's and I didn't have all A's either. I was quiet, reserved and a prime candidate elected to fall through the cracks. Yes, I did go to class most of the time, but it wasn't to get an education. It was to see how many girls showed up that day. At this time, I had no leadership, focus or direction for my life. My aunt did the best she could with me but her primary focus was the $50 on the first of the month. She even charged a $5-a-day late fee if I didn't pay on time. I had not spoken with my father since the day I left the house with my mattress. I just played along and went to school for the hell of it.

I didn't start work until 5:00 p.m., and I needed something to fill my day. The only thing that lit my fire and got me excited was playing sports. Playing football and basketball were the only two things that I could do extremely well. I would have tried out for the team, but my grades were too low and I didn't believe enough in myself to make the improvements necessary. But in my backyard, I was the king. I practiced for hours and hours and hours after school, on the weekends, in the dark, it didn't matter. For me, it was a form of release and escape from reality. In my world, everything was perfect. I controlled it, I dominated it, and no one could stop me. But outside my backyard, I was a nobody, with no power and no pride. Therefore, trying out for the school team was hopeless, but kicking butt in my backyard was the law. As the second semester of my senior year began, I had a meeting with my counselor for the first time. She informed me that if I attended night school and made up an English class I had flunked the previous semester, I could graduate even with all D's. I started to think that if I graduated from high school, I could use my high school diploma as a springboard to attend college. Maybe I could make it to the NBA or the NFL. I paid the $59 and attended night school. I passed the English class with a D. I finished my final semester of classes with three D's and one C. I graduated from Osborn High School with an overall grade point average of 1.62. I was ranked 328th out of a class of 420. However, I soon realized that a low academic performance wasn't what colleges were looking for. I called a few schools about enrollment and I even sent away for some materials for certain schools.

I was really excited about the idea of going to college until I started reading the requirements.

"All students must have a minimum Grade Point Average of 2.0. All students must take the SAT and/or the ACT. All students must have three letters of recommendation. All students must have their financial aid scholarship paperwork in the mail by May of 1991."

I met none of the requirements. After four years of high school, I had a piece of paper that said diploma on it, but it didn't have any value. I also realized that my academic skills were very low. I couldn't write a paragraph. I finished all my math classes with D's or F's. My spelling was terrible and the last book I had read with more than ten pages was Dr. Seuss' "Green Eggs and Ham." I had turned into a complete idiot in a matter of four years. The only good thing that came out of my high school diploma was the graduation ceremony. The graduation ceremony was the perfect event and opportunity that I needed to reestablish communication with my father and invite him to see me graduate from high school.

This was a good day, a day of release, a day of joy and a day of accomplishment for me. After the ceremony, my father met me outside in the front of the University of Detroit Arena and told me that he was proud of me and if I ever needed his help, I could call him. Then he reached in his pocket and pulled out my rent money, a $50 bill and said, "Good luck, but I have to go back to work." After he left, I walked over to the parking lot and sat down in my cap and gown. I thought of my grandmother and looked up to the sky.

I said, "Granny, look at your grandson now. I hope you're proud. I know my grades were bad but I promise you, I will make something out of myself. I love you."

But You Promised!!

Upon graduating from high school, there were two things that I was extremely proud of and they were not my grades or my attendance. I was extremely proud that I could dunk a ball and catch a ball. I had set a goal for myself that I was going to use my athletic ability to get out of my aunt's basement and into the penthouse. After graduation, I started practicing day and night with hopes of landing a tryout opportunity at any college I could. That summer I played and practiced with anyone who would play against me. My cousin and I frequently held 4-on-4 tournaments in our back yard with the local drug dealers, thugs and known felons from the neighborhood.

That summer, our house was a haven for every Tom, Dick and Junebug who thought they had skills and wanted to shoot hoops. On a breezy afternoon in July, my cousin, a couple of our drug dealer buddies, and my new best friend, Melvin Cokley, decided to enter into a 5-on-5 tournament that a lot of college scouts would be visiting. Although we finished fourth with the team we had, it was pretty good, considering the stiff competition. After our game was over we decided to hang around for a couple minutes more to watch some of the other games. That's when I met the man who held the key to my dream of superstardom. His name was Coach J. He was a recruiter from Fort Valley State College in Fort Valley, Georgia. Coach J pulled me to the side and told me that he liked my game and he could make me a star.

He said, "Son, has anyone ever told you that you got game? How would you like the opportunity to come down to my college and play ball for me?"

I didn't say anything, not a single word. I was in complete and total shock. Then Melvin popped me in the back of my head and said, "John, say something bro. Are you deaf? Answer the man." I gathered myself and, with the glee of a five-year-old at Christmas in the morning, said, **"Where do I sign up? What do I need to do?"** I was on cloud nine for a moment until I remembered that my grades were terrible and I knew that I had to have a 2.0 to play ball.

After Melvin and I stopped jumping up and down, I told Coach J that I really appreciated the offer but I have a small problem. My G.P.A is only 1.6. He paused for a second, looked over both of his shoulders like we were on a secret covert ghetto mission, and said, "Son, that doesn't matter. We take care of our own. All you have to do is get there, you got it!" Then he winked at me and revealed a gold tooth. Bling! Bling! He smiled showing off all of his pride and joy. Right before he jumped in his car on his way to another tournament, he told me that I could meet him on campus on September 5 and he would take care of everything else.

"Son, I promise you, you're going to have the time of your life. Free room and board, free food and a full athletic scholarship, and more importantly, you will be playing basketball and football for a great college ... See ya in September. Bling-Bling."

You talking the happiest day in my life, this was it! The very next day, I decided to take my pops up on his offer to help, if there was anything that I needed. I called him early at 5:30 a.m. that morning and before he could finish saying hello, I rattled off everything that the coach had told me.

"Pop, this coach said he was giving a scholarship and my grades don't matter and his name is Coach J and he's in Fort Valley and it's for academics. Hello, I can play football, I can play basketball. September 5, meet him, and he's taking care of it all. Hello? Hello? Did you hear what I just said?" I asked.

"Actually, son, I didn't," he said.

Of course, he wanted to have a long drawn-out conversation about my big decision.

He said, "Son, don't you think that you should spend some time thinking about this? Where's the paperwork? Who is this guy? Do you have a brochure? How do you know this is the real deal?"

Question after question after question, blah, blah, blah, and blah. I stopped him and yelled, "Pops, he promised. This is my big chance and you said if I needed your help, you would be here to help me. So are you going to help me or not?"

My father said, "Boy, who do you think you're talking to in that fashion?"

I raised my shoulders back and deepened my voice and said, "DADDY, I'M A MAN."

"What did you say, boy?" he replied.

I said, "I'M A MAN."

"I don't think I heard you correctly. Please tell me what you said again?" he said.

I raised my shoulders back again and stuck my little puny, bird chest out and said, "DADDY, I'M A MAN!" at the top of my lungs.

Finally he realized that I was serious and I was determined to fulfill my dream and he decided to assist me. All I needed was the plane ticket, which he bought, and drove me to the airport on the day of my flight. As soon as we arrived at the airport, he had a look on his face like he wanted to start up a conversation/dissertation with me. Fortunately, he didn't say a word, which was great, because if he had gotten started, I would have probably missed my flight. We unloaded my luggage and went inside to wait on my flight to be called. After waiting for a half hour, the stewardess came over the intercom, *"Flight 164 heading for Atlanta, Georgia now boarding at gate 12."* This was it, my big moment. I was leaving the nest and traveling 800 miles to pursue my dream. I stood and shook my dad's hand and walked over to the gate. I gave the stewardess my boarding pass and right before I walked through the tunnel, I turned around looked my dad square in the eyes and said, "DADDY, DON'T WORRY. I'M A MAN."

But You Promised, The Saga Continues

I arrived in Fort Valley early that afternoon. It was a beautiful sunshiny day. The temperature was about 85 degrees and there was a light fall breeze blowing. I didn't know where anything was located, but my main focus was finding Coach J. I searched for him for about twenty minutes and then I noticed a long line of about 500 students waiting to register. Out of sheer excitement, I immediately ran to the front of the line so I could register. I mean, after all, superstars don't wait in line like common folk.

"Excuse me, Miss. I'm sure you've already heard about me, so please tell me where my room is so I can go. Yeah, that's right, I'm the man from Detroit, Michigan."

"Son, I don't know who you are. Now tell me who sent

you down here?"

"Coach J sent me down here. He said that I'm the Man. So give me my room. I'm in a hurry."

The lady at the counter looked at me with a strange look on her face and started to check the names on the list. Then suddenly she stopped. "Wait, son. Did you say Coach J as in Johnson?" "Yes, that's the one," I said. "Ohhhhhhhhhhh. I see the problem now. Son, Coach J was fired last week for unknown reasons. You didn't know that? Oh well, sorry. Now get out of my line. NEXT!" At that moment I tried not to think about it, but I had a flashback of my father's original conversation coming back to haunt me.

I screamed, "WHAT THE HELL DO YOU MEAN HE WAS FIRED? SOMEBODY BETTER HIRE HIM BACK RIGHT NOW!"

Campus safety police showed up and took me to the president's office. I explained to the president my situation but he was non-sympathetic. His advice for me was to go back home and try again next year. That answer wasn't good enough for me because my pride was on the line. I could not go back home a failure. I owed it to myself. I owed it to my grandmother and I wanted to show my father that I was a man. I got a job working at McDonald's and bounced around from dorm to dorm seeking shelter for the entire first semester. During that period, I also applied for financial aid and emergency funds that the college released on occasion.

After months of working at McDonald's and waiting for my financial aid to clear, I finally was able to attend class like a regular student. There was only one hitch: because my grades were so poor from high school, the college advisor that was assigned to me recommended that I register for remedial classes. As soon as I heard that, I immediately went into a deep depression. It was official. I was a cross-country idiot, successfully stupid in not only one state but two. I registered for classes but my heart wasn't in it. My self-esteem was shot and my inner man had suffered the last blow to the head he could take. I stayed in the classes for another semester and then I decided enough was enough and I dropped out. I finished my career at Fort Valley State College with a cumulative average of 0.86.

A Wake Up Call From Death

After riding a Greyhound bus, which I refer to as the sliver mutt, for nearly 36 hours to get back to Detroit from Fort Valley, I had ample time to reflect back on my entire life. I thought about my grandmother and the promise I had made to her. I thought about the afternoon that I told my dad I was a MAN and how disappointed he was going to be of me. I thought about my middle school days and how great they were. I thought about my mother and sleeping in that old rundown warehouse. I thought about the argument I had with my dad when I was little. I thought about the day at the park when Coach J made me the promise and I even thought about committing suicide right there on the bus.

I felt I had nothing else to live for. I was the son of a drug addicted mother and a college dropout. I barely graduated from high school. I was an outcast from my father's house, a failure in the eyes of many, including myself. I was a selfish, self-centered, full of pride, bad tempered, poor black boy, beaten down mentally, emotionally and psychologically and, to make matters worse, I had cursed GOD out of my life. The only thing I had left was to give my life over to the devil.

Once I arrived back to Detroit, I took a cab to my aunt's house and the entire time, the Angel of God began to speak to me. The driver of the cab was a part-time youth pastor at a church near downtown Detroit. As soon as I got in the cab and closed the door, I looked up to tell the driver my destination. I noticed in the mirror that my eyes were bloodshot and I had this demonic look on my face that caught the cab driver's attention. He immediately pulled the cab over on the Lodge Freeway and started witnessing to me about how GOD still loved me and how good He is. Then he prayed the *Prayer of Salvation* over me and suddenly, I let out a roar that could be heard ten blocks away. It was so loud and fierce that it knocked him to the floor of the cab. I didn't know what had happened but my eyes were clear again and I felt like living. I was recharged with a full burst of energy and I felt GOD in my heart again.

At my aunt's house, I took up shelter in her basement again. The next day, I called Chili's and begged for my old job back and they hired me with no problem. After a few weeks, my life was almost back to normal, but I vowed never to go back to another school again in my life. I was going to wash dishes, play basketball and live in my aunt's basement for the rest of my life until death came to pay me a visit.

On a hot day in July, we were having one of our usual knock down, drag out, ball-until-you-fall basketball tournaments in the back yard. The cast of characters was also the same local thugs, drug dealers and street hustlers that terrorized the community. It was always a little risky playing against them but they were my cousin's friends; he grew up with them. The interesting thing about the crew was that they all played 3-on-3 basketball with thousands and thousands of dollars worth of jewelry on that would make Liberace blush.

This day, Melvin, my cousin, and I couldn't be beat. No matter what team they put on the floor, we made quick to dispose of them. Not only did we beat the teams with points, we brutalized the teams with trash talking. Guess who was the ringleader? That's right, me! I talked so much trash I could have started a riot. So what! It was my backyard and I was on top of my game. Then one of the miscellaneous thugs decided that he had heard enough from me. He snatched the ball out of my hand and threw it over the fence. Why did he do that? I had to give him my best Cassius Clay interview thrashing.

"You big dumb fool, you need to go back to school,
Boy don't you know we can't be beat,
Wait stop! I think I smell your feet,
Let me tell you something, Bo Bo,
Throwing the King's ball is a no-no,
You better not let it happen again, or you're going **to meet**
my little friend."

That was the funniest joke that I had ever told in my life. Everyone started laughing and going to the side of the house to get water from the hose. I jumped the fence, retrieved the ball and started shooting around by myself. Then all of a sudden, all of the laughter stopped and the backyard went into a complete silence. I turned around to see what was going on and there was the miscellaneous thug standing three feet away from me with a loaded .357 Magnum pointed directly at my chest. My mind told me to run, but my feet didn't move. I was screaming on the inside but my mouth wasn't making a sound. I was frozen in time waiting for death to take possession of my life. As I held that Wilson's basketball in my hand, all I could get out of my mouth to mumble was *Please don't kill me. I don't want to die. Please don't kill me.* Then:

BANG!!!

Miraculously, my angel came to my rescue again in the final nano-second of my life. A very good friend of my cousin's, named Marvin, a.k.a "Marvose," hit the miscellaneous thug's arm and caused the bullet to whiz just inches above my head and hit the garage directly behind me.

Thank you for saving my life, "Marvose." You are truly an angel from GOD. May God prosper you and your family with a long, healthy and abundant life.

RUMBLE YOUNG MAN RUMBLE

A few weeks later after the attempted assassination on my life, I changed my entire focus and direction. I was immediately taken back to the promise that I had made to my grandmother and the conversation that I overheard my second grade teacher having about me. I was determined to fulfill my promise and prove my teacher wrong. My girlfriend at the time, Christy, a 1991 University of Michigan graduate, suggested that I enroll in community college to get my life going in the right direction. I took her up on her advice and began attending class at Wayne County Community College in Detroit, Michigan in the fall of 1992. I enrolled in the Urban Teachers Program and took a job with the Detroit Public Schools as a bus attendant.

After a lot of blood, sweat and tears, I completed the associates program in May of 1995. Armed with that small success, I was promoted to Educational Technician and I transferred to Wayne State University and completed my Bachelor of Science degree in Education in December of 1996. In December of 1996, I began a career as a fourth grade classroom teacher at Spain Middle School in Detroit. In the winter of 1998, I decided to continue my education. In only three semesters, I completed my Masters degree in Educational Administration. After another year of teaching, I decided to go back to school and pursue my Educational Specialist degree in Administration and Supervision in hopes of one day completing my Doctorate degree in Education.

During this time, I also felt that it was time for me to move from the classroom to the big time, Administration. With a lot of persistence, diligence and determination in October of 2000, I was selected over 15 other candidates for the position of Assistant Principal. At age 27, I was recognized as being the youngest Assistant Principal in the history of Detroit Public Schools. Then it hit me like a lightning bolt: I can become a Millionaire by 30.

CHAPTER THREE

Release Yourself from Your Past Hurt

Take A Good Look In The Mirror

"The world is a looking glass. It gives back to every man a true reflection of his own thought."
— Thackery

How does your past hurt affect you now in your adult life? What type of person have you become because of the things that have happened to you when you were a little girl, a little boy, a teenager, a young lady, or a young man or even an adult? Did your father leave you when you were young? Were you molested as a child? Do you come from an abusive home? Did your parents give you up for adoption? Did your mother mentally abuse you? Has someone done you so wrong in your past life that it has stunted your growth and blocked you out from living a stress free life? Are you tormented and consumed by these thoughts, fears and emotions? If so, the first principle of being released from that bondage is that you, the individual, will have to take inventory and ownership of your past pain as it relates to your life and your future. Now trust me, I know this may be a difficult process but it's necessary. It's vital because it's the first door in which you have to enter and go through on your journey to your Millionaire status and stress free living. I told you in the introduction that **Millionaires do not cheat the process, remember?**

Taking Inventory

"God brings men into deep waters
not to drown them, but to cleanse them."
— Aughey

In my teenage years, when I worked for Bob & Don's Meat Market, one of the responsibilities that I had was to take inventory of the stock. That meant counting up all of the meat that we had in the entire store, including the freezer, the cooler, the deep freezers, the walk-in cooler and the meat that arrived that day. Bob, one of the owners, trained me on how to take inventory. I have to be honest, in the beginning, I didn't think something that sounded so simple required training and guidance, but it did. The first thing he taught me about taking inventory was that if you're going to do it properly and thoroughly, you had to do it after closing, when no one else is around to interrupt the process. The next step was to sit down with a sheet of paper or a notebook and visualize everything that we had in the market and write all of it down.

Now that's what we're going to do. I want you to get a pen and a notebook and find a quiet place at home, a library or any place you won't be bothered. Personally, what I like to do is drive over to the next city and rent a hotel room for about three days. Now that you have your quiet place, search deep within yourself and write down all of the deep pain that you feel inside from your past. You may ask what's the difference between deep pain and agitation? It's simple. Deep pain is pain that you have purposely tried to hide from yourself and everyone around you. It's also the pain that alters your emotional state and causes you high levels of anxiety and stress. It's the conversation that you want to have, but you are afraid to have because of its embarrassing nature. Agitation is a temporary feeling of aroused anger. Like the lady who takes too long in the checkout line, or the guy driving in front of you who won't switch lanes. Or that person who just won't stop talking in the theatre. That's agitation.

Making a List

I want to be as much of a blessing as I can. I have provided you with a personal example to help you get started:

Jonathan's Personal Inventory

I really hate the fact that my mother left my father for another man and broke up our family. I can't believe my mother would allow drugs and alcohol to take her over. How could she leave me when I was a child? Why did she love that useless guy? Why didn't my father go after her? How could my father choose Sandra over me? Why did GOD let my grandmother die?

_____

_____

_____

_____

_____

_____

_____

_____

The important issues are not grammar or spelling for you English majors. The important thing is that you get all of the pain out of you and on to the paper. That pain isn't doing you any good lying dormant and festering inside you. Once I started writing my own painful experiences down on paper, I became emotional immediately. I felt terrible for feeling terrible. At the end of my three days of writing, I cried and cried and wrote some more. I was finally released from all of the pain that had taken place in my childhood. I was finally able to forgive the people who had hurt me so badly. I forgave my mother and my father; I forgave Trevor, and I even forgave myself for being angry with GOD.

Understand that you don't have to be ashamed anymore. This is your breakthrough, your first step towards wealth and prosperity. Deep pain hinders you from receiving many of the extra blessings God has in store for your life as well as the lives of others around you. It wasn't until I released myself from my childhood pain that I was able to sit down at my computer and write this book. Now I'm helping Millions of people across the country achieve maximum success.

Forgive And Move On

*"What is required for effective change is
continuity of sincere effort to release and let go
of inefficient thought patterns from the past."*
— Howard Martin

Now that you have taken a good look in the mirror and understand the real issues of why you are not living a debt free, stress free abundant life, the next phase in this process requires that you make a conscious decision to forgive them, him, her, it, or anyone else that has caused you deep pain in the past. **This is what most people say:**

- "I can't forgive them because they caused me too much pain as a child."
- "I will never forgive them because they stole my life from me."
- "I will never forgive them because they owe me 15 years of my life back."
- "Why do they deserve forgiveness? After all they are the ones who caused me the deep pain."
- "I have experienced too much pain. They should be trying to apologize to me!"

Top Achiever, you have to understand that forgiveness is the key to the next door of that place of wealth and health.

Webster's Dictionary describes forgiveness as: *To give up resentment of, or to grant relief from payment, to pardon or absolve.*

About a year ago, I attended a Ministers Leadership Convention at my church. There was a speaker there who talked about how he was the leader or head pastor for thousands of pastors across the country. Then he shared some of the stories he encountered as he served in that position. He told one story in particular that stood out most and helped changed my life. It began with a young pastor who lived in

Ohio. He had a beautiful wife, two lovely children and a thriving congregation of 4,000 members. He was known as a pillar in his community and the surrounding suburb. One day, while he was taking out his trash and placing it on the curb in front of his house, he noticed a pornographic magazine in the trash can next to his. At first he didn't pay it any attention and he went back in the house and started getting ready for prayer. Then all of sudden, he found himself back outside in front of the house digging through the trash to find the pornographic magazine. He took the magazine out of the trash and slipped it in his bathrobe.

For the next three months, he found himself completely addicted to pornography. He would drive to nearby towns where no one knew him to buy magazines, books, sex toys and even videos. During this entire time, the pastor still went about his every day life of preaching and teaching. No one had a clue as to what was going on. Then he started having his secretary lie for him to get out of meetings so he could go out for his fix of pornography. Six months later, this same pastor was completely out of control. After preaching a Sunday service, he ran out, jumped in his car and drove straight to the porn shop. Once he realized what he had become, he decided to end his life. On one Wednesday night, he left his home and drove to the church and sat outside in the parking lot with a loaded gun to his head. As the bible study ended and the people began to leave, they noticed their pastor sitting in the parking lot, ready to end his life. Fortunately, they were able to rescue him in time, but his career was finished as a pastor. The following Sunday, he stood up in front of his entire congregation and told them about all the terrible things that he had done. He apologized to his wife and family, to the congregation, and to GOD.

The following week after losing his church, he and his family moved to another town to escape any further embarrassment. His wife was devastated by the entire event. She had to leave her beautiful home, her family and all of her friends. Not to mention, she felt that she couldn't trust her husband anymore. This pastor had caused a lot of people deep pain, especially to his wife. She wanted him to repay her for the embarrassment that he had caused their family. She also wanted him to pay for the hurt and distrust she had developed from the emotional damage she had to suffer through.

Together, they decided to seek counseling and the first thing the young pastor's wife said was that she could never forgive her husband, because he had caused her too much pain emotionally, spiritually and financially. She felt that he owed her more than an apology. Then the speaker, who happened to be their spiritual counselor, told the young wife something she couldn't believe. He said, "Young lady, the deep pain and debt that you feel your husband owes you cannot be repaid by him. That debt has already been paid through the shed blood of Jesus Christ our Lord and Savior."

Understand this, the person that has caused you deep pain cannot repay any of the debt. You can't go to any bank in America and withdraw 20 years of abusive pain, suffering or misery and repay it to anyone. What you can do, though, is forgive the person, pray for them and move on with your life. It's not worth the stress or aggravation! TRUST ME!

Keep Looking Forward

*"In front of you is where your
future lies, not behind you."*
— Anonymous

The great thing about looking forward is that it provides you the opportunity to keep your eyes focused on your goals and your vision. I find it terribly difficult for me to make any progress if I'm looking to my left or to my right, especially if I'm looking backwards into my past. Realize that the moment you start looking back into the past you begin to slow the process of you growing and arriving at your goal of living a Millionaire lifestyle. Due to all of the pain we've already suffered, we don't have time to take our eyes off the road and cause an accident. Our mission is to arrive at our destinations as safe and as expeditious as possible. Are you ready to be debt free? How about free of anxiety and stress? What about those couple of bucks that you might accumulate along the way?

I was on a crowded expressway a couple of years ago, attempting to make a 45-minute journey to the University of Michigan, when I noticed an 18-wheeler truck had rolled over in the middle of the expressway. Traffic was backed up for miles and everyone was becoming impatient. As the traffic slowly crept past the semi-trailer, I could see the skid marks and all of the damage it had caused to the cars it had hit. As I drove by, I pumped my brakes and slowed down to get a better look when the traffic behind me began to blow their horns urging me to drive on. As I drove away from this horrific accident, I had feelings of fear and curiosity come over me. I slowed down and glanced in my rearview mirror, adjusting it to better visualize the accident, bringing it back to life in my mind. Then, all of a sudden, WHAMM! I ran into the back of a bread truck and totaled my car. I never made it to my destination. In addition, I had to spend several days in the hospital, nursing my new hurts and pains.

Take my advice, keep looking forward and don't look back into the past. Realize that you do have a past and it may have been good or it may have been terrible, but your future is so much brighter!

Say this out loud with me on the count of three:
One! Two! Three!

MY BEST IS YET TO COME!

Doesn't that feel GOOD? Let's do it again.
One! Two! Three!

MY BEST IS YET TO COME!

"NOW, LET'S GO AND GET IT, BABY!"

Breathe Again

"Today is the first day of the rest of your life."
— Abbie Hoffman

The wonderful thing about the human body is that GOD designed it in such a magnificent way that it takes in oxygen automatically. This oxygen, when taken into the body, causes growth, development and life. The same body, if the path of air is obstructed in any way, can cause suffocation, asphyxiation or death. Thank God that the air we breathe is FREE. Breathing is a natural phenomenon that must take place for every individual to survive.

One of the main principles you learn in lifeguard training is when rescuing a victim, the first thing you have to do is get them to relax. Or if they have been under the water for a long period of time, you have to get them to the shore immediately. Then, regardless of what has happened, the number one priority is to get them to breathe again.

My emphasis to you, Top Achiever, is not to worry about your past or how long you've been under the water drowning. Even after the stitches, the bumps, the bruises, the alcoholism, the drugs, the molestation, the rape, the violence, the divorce, the death, the abandonment, the guilt, the embarrassment, and the deep pain, it is time for you to breathe again and take life head on. The moment you do, you will snatch victory from the jaws of defeat.

I know you may be wondering what's one of the fastest ways to get the air of freedom in your body? Good! You have developed a strong characteristic of a Millionaire: **heroism**. Heroes, this is what I want you to do, to not only breathe again, but to kick down the first door to prosperity, wealth, financial freedom and stress-free living.

<u>Breath Again Exercise</u>

I want you to take all the pages of deep pain you have completely written down and tear them up into as many tiny pieces as you can. Then take those tiny pieces of paper and place them in an envelope. Once you have all the pieces of paper inside the envelope, take the envelope and attach it to any large stone or brick that you can find. Then on a beautiful morning, when the sun starts to rise, take the brick and throw it into a large body of water. Any lake, pond, river or ocean will do. Why? Because as soon as you release that brick or that stone into the water, it's just like GOD throwing your past into the sea of forgetfulness, never to cause you any further pain, never to be analyzed again and never to be resurrected. As the brick sinks to the bottom of the body of water, lift your hands and shout as loud as you can:

I'M FREE! I'M FREE! I'M FREE! I'M FREE!

Time To Make The Change

"Change isn't change until something has changed."
— Dr. Creflo A. Dollar

Now that you're free and released, it's time to take on a new perspective in life. In order to do this, the first thing that you have to do is lay down the old you and get started on the new you. This is a process that I like to call reinventing yourself or re-imaging who you are. This means something about you has to change.

Here is a list of things you may need to change

- Your environment.
- The way you deal with people.
- Your thinking habits.
- The way you dress.
- Your relationships.
- The way you spend the majority of your free time.

I don't know what it may be for you individually, but I am certain that you need to change something. Change is a constant thing that takes place in our planet. And man is the only mammal on earth that doesn't like to change. Birds fly south for the winter, bears hibernate, and snakes shed their skin. Yet man keeps on doing the same exact thing day in and day out, never taking the time to evaluate, but always taking the time to manipulate. Why are so many people afraid to change? FEAR. Most people allow the fear of change to dictate their lives. Then you have another group of people out there who want to change the world but won't take the time to change within themselves.

My older brother lives in New York. He stands 6'4" tall and weighs about 250 lbs. One day, he walked in a store to buy a soft drink and stood in line to pay for it. The entire time he complained about how slow the line was moving; how he would run the store differently, and the owners needed to change the sign outside. Finally we made it to the front of the line; he paid the clerk with a $50 bill and forgot to get his change. Once he realized what had happened, he ran back in and told the 4'9" cashier that she didn't give him his change. She smiled at him and said, "Son, change doesn't come from me, it comes from within."

Repeat this affirmation a minimum of twice a day:

Change is a good thing!
I have now found the courage to change
I now dedicate my life to change
Change is a good thing!
I feel a change inside me now
A change that activates wealth
A change that brings better health
A change that will manifest itself
A mighty change that's not just for myself
Change is a good thing!
Change is a really good thing!

I'll prove it to you with one simple question. Wouldn't you like to change your bank account balance to __, 000,000.00. Now the first number is up to you to change. I told you *change is a really good thing!*

How To Get Started Getting Started

"It's why many fail — because they don't get started — they don't go. They don't overcome inertia. They don't begin."
— George Washington Carver

For many individuals, getting started is the most difficult part of the process. The vast majority of us can't envision finding neither the time nor the patience to get started on one of our Millionaire ideas. The everyday hustle and bustle of life consumes every waking moment of our days. Dropping the kids off at school, finding a babysitter, going to the grocery store, cooking dinner, family emergencies, paying bills, commuting back and forth to work, spending time with the husband or wife, the girlfriend, the boyfriend, the dog, the cat and the bird. Then the next day we begin the process all over again. There is so much going on in our lives that we bury our dreams deep inside us and never act on them. We have become so committed to so many other things, we often forget about ourselves. Another common reason that many individuals never get started is because of EGO.

* The Edison translation reads EGO — *Edging GOD Out.*

All of us are blessed with gifts, talents and Million dollar ideas but we just don't know where to begin. We allow our egos to get in the way and impede our forward progress in life. I remember the year that I had to take the Michigan Teacher Certification Test. A group of undergraduate students in the College of Education curriculum decided to form a study group for the upcoming exam. The group was comprised of ten individuals who were in my class at the time, eight women and two men. I didn't like the idea from the beginning. I battled with the thought of some girl trying to help me. What could any of those silly girls teach me? They must be crazy if the think they're smarter than me.

What do they know? They're in the same boat as I am. At the end of the day, I said, "Thank you, but no thanks, I'll get started on my own studying tonight at home." They said, "Fine," and I went on about my way. The funny thing was that when I got home, I didn't know where to begin. How do you study for a test that you've never seen before? How do you prepare for questions that are in Greek as far as I was concerned? After watching a couple of basketball games and drinking a few sodas, I decided to call it a night.

A couple of days went by and it was time to take the exam. Of course, I flunked it, but everyone else from that study group passed. I still didn't want their help. I took the test again the following semester and flunked it again. Now this test was the last requirement I had to fulfill to receive my teaching certificate and contract for teaching, which equates to cash, dough, moola, dinero, cheese, cheddar, loot, booty, lucre; you get the picture. A couple of months went by and I ran into three of the group members, but being the knucklehead I was, I still allowed my EGO to get in the way and I was too proud to ask for help. I took the test a third time and failed it once more. Then as graduation rolled around, I started to think what harm would it do for me to ask one of the group members for help.

With help from the other members of the group, I took the test for the fourth time and I passed it with no problem. What took me four attempts and over six months to accomplish, had I asked for help in the beginning, would probably have only taken one try.

The key to getting started is ASK FOR HELP! You know some of us just need somebody to hold our hand. Joe Frazier said, "All of us at some point and time in our lives are like the blind man standing on the corner waiting for someone to help us navigate across treacherous waters that we might not be able to navigate by ourselves."

Say this with me:

Asking for help is a good thing.
Asking for help is a really good thing.

Don't edge GOD out. Ask for help and get your ego out of the way.

Take Stock Of Your Ability

"How do you know the stock is
good stock if you don't know
what the stock is?"
— Anonymous

If a stranger were to walk up to you and say, "I'll give you a Million dollars if you can name ten things that you're good at." Would you be able to do it? I know what you're thinking. If that happened to me, I would name 500 things I'm good at, like spending money, going to the mall and making large purchases. Wait a minute — oh yeah!! Spending money and going to the mall. Did you know that the average person who is asked that question has only three to four things that they consider themselves good at. When was the last time you made a list of all the areas that you consider yourself talented in?

This is very important because in order for you to realize who you are, you have to have some sense of what you are capable of. Not only that, you give yourself what I like to call a home court advantage by taking inventory of yourself. Did you know that in most cases, other people have a better inventory of us than we do? They watch you, they study you, they even write down what you say. They know exactly what you're good at and what you're terrible at. Therefore, the first step in planning your purpose is finding out who you are.

Chapter Four

Plan Your Purpose

What Is Your Dream?

"And Joseph dreamed a dream."
— Genesis 37:5

What is your dream? If you could do one thing you have always wanted to do more than anything else in the world, what would it be? Now I didn't ask if you had the time, if the kids were asleep or how old you are. I just want to know what your dream is. If you can realize your dream and believe it, you definitely can achieve it. Most people don't believe in dreams anymore. We now live in a world that depends on luck and chance to get us where we want to go in life, which is very unfortunate because a dream is something to shoot for.

What is a dream?

- It's something to go after with everything you've got.
- It's something that will keep you up at night, excited about it.
- It's something that drives individuals to reach deep within themselves and change.
- It's something that can ignite a fire of passion in the dullest person.
- It's something that can add 20 years of longevity to your life.

- It's something that, if planned and executed correctly, can affect Millions of people.
- It's something that can give you a reason to live.
- It's something that can take you to the moon and to the stars.
- It's something that can represent you and your family for centuries to come.
- It's something that can affect the lives of Millions of children.
- It's something that can cause you to change who you are.

Most importantly, it's something that, when finished, GOD can be proud of it. Now if you're still not convinced that dreams are real, close the book right now and go to your computer and email me and I will give you a few more examples (edisonfordetroit@yahoo.com). Now what I want you to do is write down your dream. A poet once said, "Often times history is being read but it's never being written." See how important it is for you to write your dream down. You are writing yourself into the history books. Remember to list your dream (don't worry about the type of dream it is because all dreams have power).

There is a 14-year-old girl who lives in Ohio. She can prove that the power of dreams work with her **one and a half Million Dollar** bank account and her thriving Internet wholesale cookie business.

MY DREAM IS TO:

_____

_____

_____

_____

_____

_____

_____

Now that you know what your dream is, you have to do two important things to have your dream come true. First, you have to develop a vision. Second, you have to develop your goals to achieve the dream. A dream without a vision is useless and a vision without goals is even worse.

Develop Smart Goals

"The tragedy of life doesn't lie
in not reaching your goal.
The tragedy lies in having no goal to reach."
— Benjamin Mays

When I was 10-years-old, I played Detroit Police Athletic League basketball on the *Run 'n' Guns*, a 12 and under basketball team, for two years. At the very first practice of each year, coaches Mike Quick and Bobby Johnson would show up with stacks of paper and pencils. As 10 and 11 year olds, we thought that they were completely out of their minds. The coaches would pass each of us five sheets of paper and a No. 2 pencil. On the top of each page was a question. The first sheet read, *What is your goal as a team for November?* On the second sheet it read, *What is your goal as a team for December?* The third sheet read, *What is your goal as a team for January?* The fourth sheet read, *What is your goal as a team for February?* The fifth sheet read, *What is your goal as a team for March?* Once the coaches collected all of the papers, every one of them had the same exact answer, TO WIN THE CHAMPIONSHIP, which is what the average individual would say, only their answer would be to MAKE A MILLION DOLLARS.

After Coach Quick and Coach Johnson read the answers, they asked us a jarring question, "HOW ARE YOU GOING TO WIN THE CHAMPIONSHIP?" Then, of course, we sat there in the bleachers, babbling about how good we were and how much talent we had, but those answers didn't satisfy the coaches. After about ten minutes of us babbling back and forth, Coach Johnson said, "Let me tell you a thing or two about having S.M.A.R.T. goals." Then the basketball chorus sang, **"What are smart goals?"** Coach Johnson told us that the secret to having smart goals is planning. If your answer to the question, *What is a smart goal?* is "I want to make a Million dollars," that's great! However, you have to be smart about it. That's why I'm glad you purchased this book, because I get to share all of these secrets with you. Every Millionaire in America knows that smart goals are:

S pecific: Definite, having a unique relationship to something.

M easurable: To bring into comparison or competition.

A ttainable: Able to reach, arrive at and achieve.

R ealistic: Something real and the totality of real things.

T ime Activated: A period which during an action or condition exists.

It is impossible to manage what you can't measure. Your goals have to be specific, measurable, attainable, realistic and time activated. Now, if you purchased this book two days ago and said to yourself, "Wow! I really enjoyed this book I think I'm going to do something now," that's fine. However, in order for you reach your goals, you have to be specific. Take **Deborah Weinstein, 27,** for example who was specific about opening up her own staffing solutions company and grossed over **$4 Million** in 2001. Do you want to be an astronaut? Do you want to open your own company? You have to be specific just like **Ali Rizza, 21,** who opened his own retail shop selling cigars, jewelry, sunglasses and other paraphernalia and grossed over **$2 Million** in sales in 2002. Do you want to start a media relations company? You have to be specific, like **Laura Tidwell, 25,** who was very specific about starting her own media buying company and generated sales over **$25 Million.** How specific are you? What do you want to do specifically? If you're not specific, you open the door to fear, ambiguity and self-doubt.

Are your goals measurable? If one of your goals is to lose weight this year, then the first thing you have to do is jump on the scale and find out how much you weigh today. Be specific. In 30 days, weigh yourself again. That's the only way you can find out if you have lost any weight or not. If one of your goals is to start your own design firm like **24-year-old Katie Lucas,** who's company grossed over **$2 MILLION** in sales, you need to find out how fast she was able to get her company off the ground and then use that information to get started.

Are your goals attainable? I personally believe that all goals are attainable. Each of us have the power inside of us to accomplish anything we set our minds to do. Just ask **Weston Lemos, 25,** a former used-car salesman who in the year 2000 launched his major venture (public relations/investor relations), and grossed a little over **$2 Million.** Then ask **Marc Levy, 29,** and **Spence Levy, 27,** and **Jay Abramowitz, 30,** who were proclaimed "caffeine junkies," who created a winning recipe for a carbonated drink that keeps most college students up all night. Last year their company grossed well over **$1 Million.** Or how about asking **Nathan Miller, 20,** who develops and distributes software for companies. He grossed over **$2 Million** last year. You can even ask **David Reinstein, 25,** and **Melody Kulp, 25,** who created their own knock-offs of Sparkles Knock-off, Lulu's Twinkle, and grossed sales of over **$9 Million** last year. Ask **Jeff Haugen, 26,** who started a cigar bar with less than $10,000 and now grosses over **$2 Million** in sales in liquor, cigars and accessories.

Are your goals realistic? Can you wake up in the morning and run a 26-mile marathon if you've never ran three complete blocks? I doubt it!

What is realistic? Realistic is realizing that you can achieve your goals over time and diligence like the following young Millionaires:

- **Brian Robinson, 28,** who wanted to open his own "warehouse type" stores and now has four Advantages stores that gross over **$18 Million** in sales.
- **Lara Shriftman, 28,** who started her New York City-based public relations, marketing and special events firm in a $500 a month leased space. Now, she occupies a very large office and projects **$5 Million** in sales.
- **Brad Aronson, 28,** who started his own website advertising company from his bedroom and grossed over **$8 Million** last year.
- **Walter Latham, 28,** who is the entertainment mogul promoter behind the "Kings of Comedy" tour which grossed **$20 Million.**
- **Michael Branson** and **Scot Johnson, both 29,** who started a technology consulting firm from a virtual office for ten months, who now gross over **$12 Million** in sales.
- **Lief C. Larson, 25,** who started his own media service provider company and grossed over **$2 Million** last year.
- **Scott Samet, 28,** who was tired of all the junk food on the planet and created his own snack food that retails across 45 states and does over **$2 Million** in sales.
- **Tracey Milton, 28,** who loves fishing and created her own tackle and fishing accessory business doing over **$2 Million** in sales.
- **Sharon Fisher, 38,** who loved kidding around and decided to open her own costume/special event shop

that does over **$2 Million** in sales.

- **Mike Rosen, 38,** who loves sweets and created his own Mike Rosen Premium Cheesecake Ice Cream that does over **$2 Million** in sales.
- **Scott Mitic, 29,** and **Peter Mellen, 32,** who founded their own e-learning company over the Internet and generates over **$3 Million** in sales.
- **Judy Kurman, 33,** who started a costume jewelry business that does over **$2 Million** in sales.
- **Dwayne Lewis, 30,** and **Michael Cherry, 31,** who provide thousands of youth with clothing and reached over **$70 Million** in sales in 2000.

Now that you have read a list of over 25 new Millionaires who are doing extremely well, don't close the book yet. There's more to come. We need to make sure that your goals are time activated also. I promise, I will give you a chance to call your mother and tell her what you just read in a few minutes, but stay with me for a few more minutes and then call everyone you know. Time activated means setting a realistic time and plan to complete the goal that you set for yourself. All right, go ahead and make the call. You can even call me at 1-800 JEDISON or 313-283-7394 if you like.

How Big Is Your Vision?

"A blind man's world is bounded by the limits of his touch,
an ignorant man's world by the limits of his knowledge,
a great man's by the limits of his VISION."
— E. Paul Hovey

Mental visualization of what your dreams and goals are is vital for reaching maximum success and Millionaire status. You will only grow as much as your vision allows you to grow. What goals do you visualize yourself completing in the next three months? How about within the next year? What about the next three years? Visualization of yourself doing great things is a simple way to jumpstart your dreams. If you interview 100 high achievers, over 80% of them will tell you that one of the major reasons that they are doing what they are doing is because they could see themselves in their mind's eye accomplishing great and marvelous things.

That's what you have to do, future Millionaire. Understand this: the bigger the vision, the bigger the check. One key to having a great vision is to make the vision greater than you could ever imagine. You may be a housewife with two kids and visualize yourself with a chain of day care centers and that's awesome! You may be a student with poor grades, low self-esteem and a reading deficiency and see yourself doing great things in the future. Fantastic! Albert Einstein did it when he was 4-years-old. He was a slow reader.

You may be a woman with very little start up money, working a job that's making you sick and want to start a multi-million dollar company servicing hundreds of thousands of people. Awesome! Madame C.J. Walker did it with a few pennies and some hard work. You may be 60-years-old and see yourself opening up your own restaurant. Super! Guess what? Colonel Sanders did it and made Millions after age 60.

You may be a young lady who has a tremendous self-esteem problem. Everyone tells you that you're never going to be anything and you have a vision of being a television star. You know what I say, go for it! Oprah Winfrey, who happens to be a Billionaire and a national talk show host, did it. It's important for you not to back away from your vision. Don't be afraid to visualize yourself doing great things. Always remember that you were born for greatness and greatness is within you. If you can visualize yourself becoming a Millionaire, then you can!

CHAPTER FIVE

Get In The Game

Time To Play

"Only put off until tomorrow
what you are willing to die
having left undone."
— Pablo Picasso

As a little boy, Jacob sat on the floor of his father's bedroom floor listening to hours upon hours of orchestra music that his dad loved. At age 6, Jacob was so in love with the sound of orchestra music, he began to study all of the different instruments and sounds that each individual instrument made. On Saturdays, his father would take him to the House of Music, where they sold a wide variety of musical instruments. As little Jacob would run through the store, he examined each instrument and tested his young skills. He would jump up in the display window and bang the drums. Then he would run to the back of the store and strum the electric guitars. A couple of aisles over, he would try his hand at the violin. Behind the counter, he would grab a flute and blow his little heart out. Jacob would take the harp and pluck at it. Then he would grab a baton and pretend to be the conductor of an orchestra.

Little Jacob loved all of the instruments and the different sounds that they made. He didn't have a particular favorite until he discovered the mesmerizing sound of the cymbals. Jacob's dad called him over and asked him if he had ever seen an instrument like them before. Little Jacob replied, "No, how do they work?" Jacob's dad placed the cymbals on little Jacob's hands and told him to bang them together as hard as he could. Standing in the middle of the House of Music, little Jacob opened up his arms as wide as he could and banged the cymbals together. The sound was incredible to him. From that moment on, little Jacob was hooked on the sound of the cymbals. Hence, every Saturday, when Jacob's dad took him to the House of Music, the only instrument he would touch was the cymbals. For hours and hours, little Jacob would march through the store banging away at those cymbals.

On Jacob's ninth birthday, his dad decided to give him a very special gift: a trip to the orchestra. Little Jacob was so excited, he couldn't wait to hear all of the instruments playing. He dreamed of the day that he could see a live orchestra perform. Little Jacob insisted on being early so he could have the opportunity to hear the orchestra warm up. Jacob's dad arrived 30 minutes before the actual performance. As soon as the doors opened to the orchestra house, little Jacob ran down the aisle and sat in his seat waiting with immense anticipation. He could hear all of the instruments warming up in a beautiful collective sound of musical notes. The strings, the drums, the horns, and the percussion were there, but no cymbals. Jacob looked to find the cymbal player but he wasn't there.

Thirty minutes later, the curtains opened and the orchestra began to play. Then he emerged, the almighty Cymbal Player. Fifteen minutes into the performance, Jacob leaned over to his dad and asked him, "When does the cymbal player play, daddy?" His father looked at him and said, "He plays soon, son. Soon." Another 15 minutes went by and

Jacob stood up in the row and yelled, "Why isn't the cymbal player playing?" Then the usher went over to where the father and son were sitting and told them to keep it down. Jacob yelled at the usher, "Why isn't the cymbal player playing?" The usher responded just as Jacob's dad had and said, "He will play very soon, son. Just be patient." Patience was not one of Jacob's best virtues and as the curtain closed for intermission, Jacob was extremely upset.

"Daddy, why didn't he play? Why didn't he play? Why didn't he play? I want to hear the cymbals! I want to hear the cymbals! I want to hear the cymbals play, daddy!"

Then the usher walked over where they were sitting and told the father that if Jacob didn't keep the noise down, he would have to ask them to leave. Then the curtains opened again and the orchestra started playing and still no cymbals. After about 20 minutes, Jacob was beginning to believe that the cymbals would never play. Then all of a sudden, he noticed the guy with the cymbals pulling his arms back for the big finish and Jacob jumped up and yelled, "PLAY, PLAY, PLAY, PLAY, MY GOD, PLAY!"

Play your cymbals, live your life so you can give the world an opportunity to hear and see the beautiful music you have within you. Having a dream is great, having a vision is awesome, setting goals for your self is admirable, but if no one else gets to benefit from it, what good is it? I urge you, Top Achiever, to play, play, play, play, and, my GOD, play. Just think if Stevie Wonder would have never played, Miles Davis had never played, Bert Bacharach had never played, Alicia Keyes had never played, Winton Marsalis had never played, Jimi Hendrix had never played, Dizzie Gillespie had never played and Ray Charles had never played, would the world be the same, musically?

Get Your "BUT" Out Of The Way

*"Ninety-nine percent of failures are
from people who have a habit of
making excuses."*
— George Washington Carver

Have you ever thought about doing something different or new with your life? Maybe starting a new career, going to school to further your education, getting the training that's required for you to open your own business, quitting your job so that you can live the dream that's been burning deep inside you for over a decade? Then you finally make up your mind to go for it and before you can take another breath, a big "BUT" comes out of your mouth. You actually begin to minimize your dream and destroy the possibility of reaching your goals. Has this ever happened to you? Good. Then I don't feel so bad, because I used to practice this defeating technique in my life on a daily basis.

The word "BUT," that pops out of your mouth so freely, is just another form of excuse for not having the guts or the backbone to go after your dreams, goals and visions. Millionaires are not wimps and they don't make excuses. They make things happen. Millionaires are also people who don't look for excuses, they look for solutions. A young farmer living in Montana dreamed of being rich and expanding his operation across the country. One day he and a buddy were sitting on his front porch when the phone rang. It was a national distributor who wanted to buy $3 Million worth of corn from him. This was just what the farmer had dreamed. The only problem was that this young farmer grew potatoes and not corn. Now he could have made all kinds of excuses for not filling the order. *I do want to be rich, "BUT" I only grow corn. I would try to fill the order, "BUT" it's too much. I'm so glad you called, sir, "BUT" I can't help you.* You know what the farmer did? He got his "BUT" out of the way and accepted the challenge. He knew two things: one, he was capable and, two, he wanted to be rich. So he immediately began working on a solution. He contacted a few of his local farmer buddies and made a deal with them, filled the order and cleared over $1 Million in profit. Then he took some of his profit and started growing potatoes.

Here Are Ten Excuses For Failure.
- I would go look for a job, BUT I'm tired of looking.
- I would go back to school, BUT it's too expensive.
- I would pursue my dream, BUT no one believes in me.
- I would quit my job, BUT I can't right now.
- I would love to do what they are doing, BUT I'm not good enough.
- I might be good at that, BUT who am I?
- I can see myself living my dream, BUT how?
- I would pray and ask GOD for help, BUT He's probably busy.
- I would save some money, BUT I just can't stop spending.
- I would try to make a Million dollars, BUT, come on, that's crazy.

How many of these top ten excuses are you guilty of? If your answer is one or all of them, don't worry. This book will help you get your "BUT" out of the way. Repeat after me: NO MORE EXCUSES! Louder! NO MORE EXCUSES! Stop making excuses and live your life. Go after your dreams and goals as if your life depended on it. Why? Because it does!

Here Are Ten Reasons To Stop Making Excuses.
- **Tarina Tarintino, 30,** opened her own costume and jewelry design business when everyone thought she couldn't do it and last year her company did over **$5**

Million in sales.

- **Phil Shawe, 30,** who loves language, dreamed of being a professional translator and started his company in his dorm room with less than $500. Now he has 14 offices and a firm worth over **$15 Million.**

- **Tony Hawk, 31,** who, as a kid, loved to skateboard, now grosses over **$12 Million** a year in clothing sales and endorsements.

- **Suzanne Lowe, 30,** a golf player, was tired of the available line of women's golf clothes. She started her own line of golf apparel and earned **$1 Million** in sales last year.

- **Mark Lee, 37,** set out to answer the question for thousands of babies. He started a company that creates a time capsule for children to look back over their lives and he's not looking back because he made over **$2 Million** in revenue last year.

- **Douglas Stewart, 32,** who was a school teacher who left his job to travel to the Brazilian Amazon jungle where he discovered a market for rain forest fruits. He started a company that manufactures exotic sorbets with ingredients from the rain forest. He's not monkeying around because he earned over **$2 Million** in sales last year.

- **Greg Brophy, 33,** sat in his office at work and found his paper shredder fascinating. He thought it would be kind of fun to shred paper for a living. Then he started Shred-it America Inc. and he brings in about **$22 Million** a year shredding paper for large companies.

- **Andrew Zenoff, 31,** was a struggling actor who had hit rock bottom. He moved in with a friend who had a child and noticed that she was struggling with holding her baby while she breast fed. So he came up with a solution, a support pillow that allows mothers to breast feed in comfort. This baby-loving idea allowed him to gross over **$2 Million** in sales last year.

- **Rhonda Lashen, 34,** whose fortune became bright when she designed fortune cookies with little cute fortunes inside them for executives and insurance company conventions. Her next fortune cookie told her, "You will make over **$2 Million** this year," and she did!

- **Ray Barnes, 34,** discovered the dead body of his grandfather with blood and brain matter all over the grass. He was horrified, but he decided to clean it up. This lead him into crime scene clean up and he cleans his way to over **$2 Million** a year.

- **Greg Maples, 34,** is a former Marine who loved burritos in high school. Fresh out of the Marines, he couldn't find any good burritos that satisfied him. Then he decided to create his own. Now he has an enchilada of a bank account earning over **$12 Million** in food sales per year.

Become A Researcher

*"The artist is nothing without the gift,
but the gift is nothing without work."*
— Emile Zola

If you have made the decision to become a Millionaire, then you have to also make a commitment to put in some work. Think of it like this, here's a golden opportunity for you to be nosy. Dig up stuff, discover secrets, hear all of the gossip, find out what the real deal is, get the goods on the competition, play I Spy, Columbo, Inspector Gadget, Nancy Drew, Kojak, and Scooby Doo. That's what research is: learning how to be nosy. Research is also designed to help aid and assist you in cultivating and living out your goals and dreams.

Webster describes "research" as *careful or diligent search; a study aimed at discovery and interpretation of new knowledge.* This discovery quest, which is a necessary requirement, can save you valuable time and money. Suppose you had an idea or a dream to open up your own hotel. One day you're driving along and notice a perfect location that's for sale. Next, you take your life savings of $50,000 and work diligently for six months, sticking to goals, holding a vision of you completing the dream and overriding all of the "BUTs" that come up.

A few months later, your dream has now manifested and you're excited. The last step is to have the city inspectors come out, inspect the building and the property. You're so confident that everything will go well that you take out a loan for $5,000 to have the biggest grand opening ever. Then the building inspector informs you that it is impossible for you to open your business because the land is contaminated. A good researcher will minimize these types of mistakes that could be devastating to your mental, personal and physical state. No matter what your dream or goal is, before you run out and lose your shirt, do the research. A wise man once said, "The only thing on the planet that's original in modern day times is the bible. Everything else is a copy." Find out who's doing what you want to do and use that information to help you reach your Millionaire status.

Examples of Profitable Research:

A	B	C
McDonald's	Burger King	Wendy's
Hollywood Video	Blockbuster	Movie Mania
2Pac	Ja-Rule	Master P
Ford	General Motors	Chrysler
Apple	Gateway	Compact
Baskin Robbins	Dairy Queen	Mr. Softy
Holiday Inn	Red Roof Inn	Motel 6

What you begin to notice is that company A, B, and C provide the same service and all of them are profitable. Why? Because some smart person decided to research one of them, emulate their style, and study their success formula.

*"Is there anyone so wise as to learn
by the experiences of others?"*
— Voltaire

Find A Captain To Show You How To Be A Captain

"Very few men are wise by his own counsel,
or learned by his own teaching. For he that was
only taught by himself had a fool for his master."
— Ben Johnson

If your true desire is to become successful and wealthy beyond belief, then it would be wise for you to find an individual who has already become successful and wealthy. It's funny that the people with the most success advice are also the same people who are living from paycheck to paycheck and are $500 from being evicted and erased off the planet. Here's something to think about. If you were stranded on a desert island with ten people and, within the next 48 hours, a hurricane was coming to wipe you out, which person would you ask for help to make it off the island to safety? The butcher, the baker, the dancer, the florist, the college student, the pregnant woman, the tall guy with the funny mustache, the taxi driver, the bum who sat outside the gas station, or the native of the island who owned three ships docked only a few feet away? I hope you answered the native, because the native knows exactly how to get to the place you're trying to go, which is to safety. And safety translates into security, which translates into Millions. Now go out and find a native of Millions and let them help you get to safety.

Webster's definition of *captain: a commander, a commissioned officer, a leader and a dominant figure.*

How To Serve Your Captain

"A man who can't follow a leader
will never be a man that any
one follows."
— Bishop Keith A. Butler

What I'm about to share with you now is very unpopular to the *Me! Me! Me! How much? How soon? And what time?* society that we live in today. Not very many people even think to take this route to success, but it's a path that every Millionaire that I have had a conversation with has traveled. Once you find your captain to teach you how to be a captain, you have to do the big "V" and the "V" does not stand for vexing, which brings trouble, distress and agitation. Your big "V" stands for VOLUNTEERING.

Before you close the book and throw it across the room, give me a moment to explain. Most people believe all Millionaires woke up one day and received a phone call and the lady on the other end said, "Please pick up your Million dollars today or else." No, that's not the way it happens. The majority of Millionaires today have had to sacrifice, volunteer, step outside of their comfort zone, eat things that they didn't like, go places they didn't want to go, smile when they felt like crying, and stand around and wait on their captains to give them another order. I told you in the beginning, Millionaires do not cheat the process and they won't allow the process to be cheated. The Millionaire status is an exclusive club with rules, regulations, guidelines and procedures. I guarantee you, if you chose a captain and volunteer, the experience will be the equivalent of a college education and more. Always remember that wealth begins with sacrifice and ends with a lot of perks.

Shut Up And Listen!

*"Daniel quiet, remember I am the master
teacher and you are the student."*
— Mr. Miagi

One of the biggest mistakes I could have made in my life was trying to out talk and outshine my captain. In my short lifetime, I have been extremely blessed to find some of the best captains to lead me. Once I reached the point that I was ready to make the transition into Millionaire status, I began seeking out Millionaires to teach me. I found myself in an elevator with a young gentleman who was a Multi-Millionaire that really loved GOD and life. His name was La-Van Hawkins, CEO of the $300 Million Hawkins Food Group Corporation. What better combination could a captain have for me to learn from. As I diligently volunteered to get his car washed, pick up his cleaning and do some of his grocery shopping, I proved myself as a young man with serious goals about life and my pursuit of wealth.

After six months of serving my new captain without error, he decided that it was time for me to be promoted. One Saturday night, after I had made sure his shoes were shined for the week, he told me that he was giving me an opportunity to accompany him and one of his business partners for dinner in New York. I was instructed to pick him up from his house by 5:00 p.m. so we would make it to the airport in time to take his private jet. Once we were aboard the jet, my mouth just took over. I tried to lead the conversation by showing how smart I was. I gave them advice on how to make more money. I even attempted to tell them how to run their businesses more effectively.

After about 30 minutes of my mindless babbling, my captain, Mr. Hawkins, looked at me and yelled, *"Jonathan, would you shut up; I'm trying to tell you how to make money. I've already made hundreds of Millions of dollars. What about you?"* Needless to say I didn't say another word for the rest of the evening. Take my advice, I'm speaking from first hand experience: **Shut Up and Listen!**

Captains don't become captains because they're stupid. A captain becomes a captain because they know how to listen, take notes and generate wealth!

Have You Made The Commitment?

*"If a man hasn't discovered something
that he will die for, he isn't fit to live."*
— Martin Luther King, Jr.

To live fully and successfully, we all must commit to something. Your vision, dreams and goals will be impossible for you to achieve if you fail to make a commitment. The first commitment that you have to make is a commitment to yourself. Say this with me, "IF IT'S TO BE, IT'S UP TO ME!" That's right, it's up to you because no one else is going to live your dream for you. You're going to have to do it yourself. Starting with a commitment of time, energy, hard work and hustle. In order to have something different for your life tomorrow, you have to make a commitment that you're going to do something different in your life today. No man has ever accomplished anything great without first making a commitment to it.

Many people miss out on opportunities for greatness, wealth and stress free living because they fear failure. Don't worry about failure, just commit. Once you make a commitment, providence moves too. Providence means all the acts of GOD and divine guidance will assist you in making your dream a reality. The power of commitment will short circuit fear and cause it to help you instead of hurt you.

It wasn't until Jesse Owens made the commitment to his track career that he was able to break the heart of Adolf Hitler by breaking the world record of the men's 100-meter run in 10.2 seconds in the 1936 Olympic Games in Berlin.

It wasn't until Shirley Chisholm made the commitment to freedom and justice that she was able to become the nation's first black congresswoman of New York City.

It wasn't until Colin Powell made the commitment to his military career that he was able to serve as Chairman to the

Joint Chiefs of Staff in 1989 and went on to become the most powerful black man in the history of the White House, second in command to the President of the United States of America.

It wasn't until a curly haired boy by the name of Thurgood Marshall made a commitment to his education that he was able to accept the President of the United States' offer to the post of U.S. Solicitor General and become the first black man to hold the post, then move on to the U.S. Supreme Court to become the first black justice in the court's 178-year history.

It wasn't until Fredrick Douglas made a commitment to himself to be free that he was able to go on to publish a best-selling account of his life.

It wasn't until Dr. Ben Carson made the commitment to science that he was able to bring himself from D's in grade school to the leading neurosurgeon in the country.

It wasn't until Martin Luther King, Jr. made the commitment to GOD that he was able to change a nation and touch the lives and hearts of Millions.

Top Achiever, I urge you to make the commitment because, once you do, you will be surprised at what great and marvelous things you can accomplish.

Repeat this affirmation every day before you begin your journey:

I COMMIT MYSELF TODAY TO BECOMING SUCCESSFUL.
I RECOGNIZE THAT SUCCESS IS A PROCESS,
NOT A DESTINATION.
I WILL DISCOVER MY DREAMS AND
DO WHAT I CAN TO KNOW MY PURPOSE IN LIFE
THAT I MAY GROW AND REACH MY
MAXIMUM POTENTIAL.
ALTHOUGH THE ROAD MAY GET BUMPY
AND IT MAY FORCE ME TO LEARN A NEW WAY
OF LOOKING AT LIFE,
I WILL DO WHATEVER IT TAKES TO
PERSERVERE.

Have You Prayed?

"Tomorrow I plan to work,
work from early until late. In fact, I have
so much to do that I shall spend the
first three hours in prayer."
— Martin Luther King Jr.

Top Achiever, GOD wants nothing less for you than excellence, wealth, peace, love and a prosperous debt-free life of abundance. Understand that GOD is an all-knowing GOD. He sees and hears everything. He knows that you want to be successful. He knows that you want to live a stress-free life and He knows that you may be afraid to take the plunge. He even knows what you're going to do before you do it. But does He know your voice? Do you have communication with Him on a regular basis through prayer? Prayer gives you access into GOD's grace for your life and without it you will never prosper.

All Millionaires practice the power of prayer because we know that praying to GOD releases Dunamis power, Kratos power, grace, mercy, protection, energy, favor, wisdom, money, wealth, healing, joy, goodness, sufficiency, help, strength, supernatural ability and wholeness with nothing missing and nothing broken. Do you realize what you're missing out on if you don't pray? Now I want to provide you with prayer scriptures direct from the mouth of the author and the creator of the world, God Almighty!

"Evening, and morning, and at noon, will I pray." **(Ps. 55:17)**

"And in the morning, rising up a great while before day, he went out, and departed into a solitary place and they prayed." **(Mark 1:35)**

122

"When I am weak, and then am I strong." (2 Cor. 2:10)

"And being in an agony, he prayed more earnestly." (Luke 22:44)

"He will regard the prayer of the destitute, and not despise their prayer." (Ps. 102:17)

"When my soul fainted within me...my prayer came in unto thee..." (Jonah 2:7)

"My strength is made perfect in weakness." (2 Cor. 12:9)

"But thou, when thou prayest, enter into thy room, and when thou hast shut the door, pray to thy Father who is in secret; and thy Father who seeth in secret shall reward thee openly." (Matt. 6:6)

"Search me, O GOD, and know my heart: try me, and know my thoughts. And see if there be any wicked way in me..." (Ps. 139:23-24)

"For GOD is in heaven, and thou upon Earth: therefore let thy words be few." (Eccles. 5:2)

"Ye ask, and receive not, because ye ask amiss..." (James 4:3)

"Ask, and it shall be given you; seek, and Ye shall find: knock, and it shall be opened unto you:" (Matt. 7:7)

"Let your request be made know unto GOD." (Phil. 4:6)

"But let him ask in faith." (James 1:6)

"And whatever ye shall ask in my name, that will I do." (John 14:13)

"The effectual, fervent prayer of a Righteous man availeth much." (James 5:16)

"If we ask anything according to his Will, he heareth us."
(1 John 5:14)

"Show me your ways, O Lord, teach me your paths; guide me in your truth and teach me, for you are GOD my Savior, and my hope is in you all day long." **(Psalms)**

"Casting all your care upon Him; for he careth for you."
(1 Pet. 5:7)

"Whatever things ye desire, when ye pray, believe that you receive them, and ye shall have them." **(Mark 11:24)**

"May the Lord answer you when you are in distress; May the name of the GOD of Jacob protect you, May he send you help from the sanctuary and grant you support from Zion." **(Psalms)**

"The king shall joy in thy strength, O Lord; and in thy salvation how greatly shall he rejoice! Thou hast given him his heart's desire, and hast not withheld the request of his lips." **(Ps. 21:1-2)**

"And it came to pass in those days, that he went out into mountains to pray, and continued all night in prayer to GOD." **(Luke 6:12)**

"These all continued with one accord in prayer and supplication, with women, and Mary the mother of Jesus, and with his brethren." **(Acts 1:14)**

"Rejoicing in hope; patient in tribulation; Continuing instant in prayer." **(Rom. 12:12)**

The scriptures that I have provided are powerful tools for activating success in your life. Refer to them as much as possible because they will be a definite blessing to your life. Start your day with prayer, continue your day with prayer and end your day with prayer. A wise man once said, "True prayer always receives what it asks for and something much better."

What Do You Love?

*"I would rather fail at something
that I love, than to be good at
something that I hate."*
— Anonymous

There was a Harvard study conducted involving 1,000 college students from across the country. The interviewer asked each one of them the same question, "When you graduate are you going into your chosen field because of the love you have for it? Or are you going into your field of choice for the money?" Eighty-seven percent of the students recently interviewed said for the money and the other 13% said for the love. The astounding fact about this study was that 20 years later, these same students were interviewed again. Two of the students who had responded that they were going into their chosen field for the love of it managed to accumulate net worths that were twice the amount of the entire group of students who responded for the money.

Likewise, a Yale study, conducted a few years ago, interviewed 180,000 Americans. These people were asked the simple question of "Do you like your job?" Over 95% responded in a daunting NO! How important is it for you to find what you love? Listen to these statistics. AAA Insurance Company released a study that showed how many accidents occur in a year, a month, a day and what time of day the accidents most likely occurred. Do you think you know the answer? The report stated that most accidents in America take place between 6:00 a.m. and 7:00 a.m. on Monday mornings during rush hour traffic. Why? It's simple: these people don't love their jobs. Therefore, they drive recklessly and without caution. Just look at the increased number of road rage incidents, which have occurred within the last five years. The numbers are astronomical! People are driving like maniacs to get to jobs they hate, then they turn around and drive like maniacs to get away from their jobs.

How many times has this happened to you? You're driving along minding your own business and some maniac flips you the bird because you're driving the normal posted legal speed. You know why he did it? Because he hates his job! He feels that he is underpaid and overworked. Deep down he wants to strangle his boss. Instead of doing something that he loves, he settled for doing something just to pay the bills. This terrible choice he made also opened the door to stress, anxiety, worry, frustration and a feeling of low self-worth.

One day, two little boys were sitting on a porch in the backyard. The first little boy looked over to the other one and said, "Hey, I bet you my dad is faster than your dad." The other little boy said, "No he's not! My dad is so fast, he can throw a football down the street and catch it before it hits the ground." Then the first little boy said, "Well that's nothing, my dad can shoot a bow and arrow and catch the bow before it hits the target." The second little boy responded, "Well my dad is so fast that he can outrun a car." The first little boy said, "My dad is so fast, he can outrun a speeding train." The second little boy stopped and said, "Well my dad is sooooo fast, he can go up on the roof, drop a quarter and run down ten flights of stairs and catch it before it hits the ground." Then the first little boy said, "Oh yeah! Well my dad is sooooo fast, he can get off work at 5:00 p.m. and be home by 4:15 p.m."

Finding out what you love and going after it will provide you with many years of good health, happiness and wealth beyond belief.

Here are five people who love what they do:
- **Mike Manclark, 35.** Mark loves airplanes. In fact, he can tell you what type of airplane is flying overhead

without even looking. Mark turned his hobby of repairing and restoring planes into a **$26 Million** business.

- **Jill Nadine, 36.** Jill loves selling all-natural, handmade body cream in little ceramic jars that she designed for herself. Who would have guessed that her little jars would have caused her to buy big buckets to hold the **$2 Million** she made last year.
- **Daniel Grossman, 39.** Daniel, as a child, loved to play with toys and he eventually landed himself a job at Toy R Us. Then he decided to start his own toy line. Who's playing now? Daniel is playing with **$5 Million** plus that he earned last year.
- **Lisa Carson, 37,** loves to work at home and work on the computer. She loved both so much that she quit her job and started her own computer training service from her living room. Now she's babysitting over **$3 Million** in annual sales.
- **David Watkins, 31.** David loved hip hop music, clothes and the entire vibe. So he started an advertising and marketing firm with $2 in his pocket in his basement. Now he's bopping his head to the tune of over **$4 Million** in revenue a year. Not too shabby for a basement operation.

All of these young Millionaires have one thing in common: they love what they do and they do it well because they love it. A sports interviewer once asked Dwayne Johnson, "The Rock," "How did you become the People's Champion in the World Wrestling Federation Championship and the most electrifying wrestler in world?" He paused, raised his eyebrow, and said, "It's simple, Jabroni, I love kicking ass and taking names."

CHAPTER SIX

Control Your Emotions

Control Your Emotions

"Any man that allows anger,
stress, and strife to interfere
with his Million Dollar Mission
deserves to be broke and stressed."
— Jonathan Edison

As a young man growing up, I experienced a lot of pain that caused me to develop a temper, as you already know. If you decided to skip to this chapter without reading about me, STOP!! RIGHT NOW!! Just kidding! See I told you I had a temper. Seriously, my childhood pain played a huge role in me developing an inferiority complex about myself. Deep within myself, I knew I was an intelligent kid, but everyone knew me as a total screw up. The pain of inadequacy transpired into me challenging anyone to a verbal match of trash-talking.

This was one of the ways that I could hide what people thought of me and show the world that I was brave, strong and fearless. Whenever I stepped on a court to play basketball, I would immediately attempt to intimidate whoever was guarding me. It didn't matter if my opponent was taller than me, shorter than me, heavier than me, or even a girl. I talked smack to them all. The majority of the time I would even threaten my opponents with physical abuse if they tried to steal the ball from me. I was so fierce that, even in Little League, my teammates nicknamed me little C.B., Charles Barkley. I reveled in the idea that I was a 14-year-old intimidator, until my trash-talking and intimidating ways cost my team the Championship.

During the season playing basketball in the Police Athletic League (P.A.L), the games were really tight and intense. Nerves were running high and the coaches were popping blood pressure pills like aspirins. My team managed to make it to the playoffs and even into the final round to the Championship game.

During the game, I was being my usual friendly self, cursing out players and running into them with elbows on purpose. Then, on one particular play, a guy from another team decided that he was bigger and more intimidating than me. He was guarding me under the basket and threw a cheap shot at me, hitting me in the throat. Why did he do that to little C.B.? The very next play, I ran down the floor as he dribbled the ball towards me and crashed into him so hard that it knocked the wind out of him and he passed out.

The coach from the other team went nuts. He ran out on the floor after me and I let him have it too. As soon as he tried to grab me, I slipped around to the back of him and grabbed him around his neck and wrestled him to the ground. Then the referee, an off-duty police officer, tried to get me off the coach and I punched him in the chest. I was completely out of control, my attitude was terrible and I thought it was one of my better virtues. After the melee subsided, the off-duty cop came over and slapped a pair of stainless steel handcuffs on me.

Minutes later, he escorted me down the stairs and out of the door to a holding tank, located next door to the gym. When I got there, all I saw were hardened criminals, staring at me as though they wanted to have me for a little tasty snack. Several hours later, my coach came down to have me released and he gave me some good news and some bad news. The good news was that we had won the game and the other coach didn't want to press charges. The bad news was that we had to forfeit the game because of my unsportsman-like conduct, which translated into my bad attitude and unstableness being the cause of a 15-man team and two coaches not to have the opportunity to participate in the championship game. I felt terrible because the whole team had worked extremely hard for the entire season.

I went down in history as little C.B., the Championship Killer, who couldn't control his emotions. Because of this, many people were affected by my feelings of inadequacy. Unknowingly, I was sabotaging my own self-worth by allowing my emotions to consume me and letting my anger take over without giving any account to how, what or who I affected around me. I have learned over time that emotions are very dangerous if the owner doesn't have them on a short leash and trained. Emotions encompass a lot of feelings. They can come back to bite you and, in some cases, they will even do you great bodily harm. In essence, control your emotions. Don't allow your emotions to control you. Individuals who allow their emotions to control them can suffer a lifetime of pain, hurt and poverty.

Toughen Up!

"Genius is the capacity to take infinite pains."
— Thomas Carlyle

All Top Achievers, Millionaires, men and women of great accomplishments in their time are some of the toughest people in the universe you would ever want to meet and know. If you plan to be a Millionaire, you had better get ready to go into battle. Oh, I'm sorry! I didn't tell you in the beginning of this book that becoming a Millionaire requires you to put on armor. I sincerely apologize with all my heart for not mentioning that. Yeah, right!!! You will never become a Millionaire, Top Achiever, or anyone who does anything great in the universe if you are, excuse the term, a "wussy." Stop being so sensitive to every little thing that happens to you.

I had a friend call me complaining of how the bank turned her down for a loan to make improvements to her restaurant. I asked her, "Are you out of business?" She said, "No!" I said, "Well, don't complain, find another way to get the money." There's an old saying, "One monkey don't stop no show." It's true! As you grow and begin to develop your dream you are going to experience a few setbacks.

Below is a list of obstacles you may experience:
- People stealing from you.
- Late deliveries.
- Someone trying to steal your idea and claim it as his or her own.
- Days when you just can't see the light.
- Nights when the people who owe you money won't return your call.
- The word "NO" when you need it most.
- Deceitful people.
- People hating you for no reason.

- People gossiping about you.
- Reading negative things about yourself in the news-paper.
- Unbalanced books.
- Missed flights.
- Missed opportunities
- Getting fired.
- A sense of resentment from your family.
- Doubters who want to see you fail.
- Individuals who spend your money like it's theirs.
- People trying to hang around you for a free ride.
- Someone breaking into your business.
- Bounced checks.
- A tax audit from the government.
- Public embarrassment.
- A feeling of loneliness.
- A feeling of fear.
- A moment of madness.
- A day when you feel like you've had enough.
- Moments of mental anguish.
- Days of discontentment.
- Nights of crying yourself to sleep.
- Important faxes that never made it.
- Losing hundreds, thousands and even Millions of dollars because of someone else's mistake.
- Lawsuits against you.
- Expensive attorney fees.
- Credit card fraud.
- All of these things if you plan to follow the road of becoming a Millionaire.

WOW! I don't know if I want to take that trip. I think I'll stay home and get some rest. Get that negative thought out of your mind and TOUGHEN UP!!

Every experience that I listed also has a counter effect. You may become:

- Wiser, stronger, better, more efficient, careful, attentive.
- Relaxed, sharp, brighter, more intelligent, and easier to get along with.
- Wealthier, fruitful, wise, a genius, tough, strong, mighty, a captain.
- More diligent, less wasteful, more prayerful, a better problem solver.
- A solution maker, a leader, a giver, a stronger backbone, encouraged.
- Fearless, powerful, an icon, a man or woman greatly respected.
- An individual people look up to, a better businessperson, a deeper thinker.
- A producer, a better reader, a good judge of character, a great money manager.
- An awesome planner, a phenomenal time manager, and, for some of you, you may even become more attractive to the opposite sex. It's true, people who are leaders have a magnetism about them that is irresistible. NOW DON'T YOU FEEL BETTER?

Don't Stress

*"The components of anxiety, stress, fear, and
anger do not exist independently of you in the
world. They simply do not exist in the physical
world, even though we talk about them as if they do."*
— Dr. Wayne Dyer

About five years ago, I stressed about everything until I became the new and improved Jonathan Edison. Where are my socks? Who has my book? Where are we going? Do you think it's going to work? How much is it? Who's paying for it? Why do I have to go? Why is she looking at me? Why is he looking at me? Who's coming down the street? How will I pay for school? Will I ever get married? How am I going to be successful? Will I have enough time? Is it because I'm black? Will her parents like me? Should I apply? Was I loud enough? Did I talk too much? Is my line in the front of my head straight? Am I tall enough? Will my car start? Am I paying too much? You name it, I stressed about it. I worried about so many things that I forgot what I was worrying about in the first place. After a few months of constant worrying, I worried if I wasn't worrying.

This type of anxiety and stress in your life will open the door to a host of illnesses to attack your body. Did you know that you could worry a hole in your stomach? That's right, you can. This is where an ulcer develops. They are caused in your body by constant worrying and often discharge pus that festers and corrupts like an open sore. Allow me to share these statistics with you. Did you know that 90% of what you worry about happening never happens? Think about this! Try to remember the last thing you worried about, no matter how insignificant or serious it may have been. Did it happen? Or did you just forget about it because it never happened?

Stress is just another form of the enemy attempting to

attack your mind and body. Have you ever noticed a person who has lost all of their hair due to stress? What about someone who has lost his or her job because they couldn't take the pressure, when, in fact, it's not the pressure of the job. It's the individual worrying about the pressure of the job that causes him or her to malfunction.

Stress can also cause tumors, cysts, knots, lumps, bumps, skin rashes, kidney failure, swollen feet, blurred vision, chest pains, bleeding ulcers, erectile dysfunction, vaginal dryness, nose bleeds, sweaty palms, permanent damage to the brain, liver damage, smoking, drinking, drug use, paranoia, schizophrenia, dry mouth, heart attacks, back pain, neck problems, strokes, arthritis, irregular heart beats, blood clots, ear infections, colds, shortness of breath, debt, poverty, illness and death. So I'm telling you for the last time, DON'T STRESS OR WORRY; 90% OF EVERYTHING YOU WORRY ABOUT NEVER HAPPENS ANYWAY.

Develop A Positive Mental Attitude

"The greatest discovery of my generation
is that a man can alter his life simply by
altering his attitude of mind."
— William James

In today's world, it's more important than ever that we develop a positive mental attitude about life, our dreams, our aspirations and our goals. Without the power of positive thinking, we become like a flower that has withered and died because it had not received enough sunlight. Are you providing your spirit and mind with enough sunlight? How about the people who you come into contact with? Do they feel your powerful brightness when you greet them? Are other people affected by your positive attitude? Or are people scattering when they see you coming because you're such a negative person? Are you the type of person who rehearses the statement, "I'm just not a morning person?" Do you find something wrong with everything? Are you the one who complains all the time? Are you the one who finds fault in everyone else's personality? Are you too lazy to say "Excuse me?" Do you look for things to go wrong? Are you so negative that if we put you in a dark room, you would develop?

Throughout my teaching career, I had the wonderful opportunity to meet a lot of great people and a lot of not so great people. That's a story for another day! What I found is that most of the people I came into contact with had a terrible mental attitude. Everyone in the school was grumbling and mumbling about something. The parking lot is too far from the door, the bathroom needs to be bigger, these kids don't have any respect, parents these days don't do anything to help their kids, day in and day out. They complained and complained and finally, one day in the middle of one of the complaining sessions, I couldn't take it anymore. I jumped up and shouted, "Why don't you quit? No one is holding you here. Please leave and stop bringing my day down." Say this with me:

NEGATIVITY IS CONTAGIOUS
BUT I AM FREE FROM IT.
ALL OF MY THOUGHTS
FROM THIS POINT ON
WILL BE POSITIVE THOUGHTS.
NEGATIVITY IS CONTAGIOUS
BUT I AM FREE FROM IT.
ALL OF MY WORDS
FROM THIS POINT ON
WILL BE POSITIVE WORDS.
NEGATIVITY IS CONTAGIOUS
BUT I AM FREE FROM IT.
FROM THIS POINT ON
ALL OF MY ACTIONS
WILL BE POSITIVE ACTIONS.
NEGATIVITY IS CONTAGIOUS
BUT I AM FREE FROM IT.
FROM THIS POINT ON
ALL OF MY ACTS
WILL BE POSITIVE ACTS.
NEGATIVITY IS DEAD
AND FROM THIS POINT ON
POSITIVITY TAKES OVER
ME!

I'm going to share a few secrets with you that I use to keep myself positive.

The first thing I do in the morning when I wake up is thank God for another day of life, my health and the ability to praise Him. The reason I do this first is because I know that without Him, there would be no me. Simple, right? Then the next thing I do is go down the list and thank Him for each and every body part, joint, muscles and rhythmic mystery that takes place in my body without me even being aware of it. Then I get down on my knees and pray for other people and their families. Why? Have you been to a hospital, jail, halfway house or mental institution lately? There are a lot of people who are a lot worse off than I thought I was.

After I pray for others, I pray for myself and I ask God to strengthen me and keep my mind and thoughts on good things, increase my territory, not allow me to bring hurt, evil or destruction to anyone and to guide my footsteps in the way he would have me to walk. Then, I tell my Angel exactly what I need him to do for the day. Finally, I read ten to 15 pages of something positive — scripture, affirmations, positive quotes or speeches given by great men. This is all before 6:00 a.m. and once I'm finished, my battery is charged up for the day to spread positive energy and keep negative energy away.

DOMINATE Fear

"Fear is the most devastating
of all human emotions.
Man has no trouble like the
paralyzing effects of fear."
— Paul Parker

What is fear?

Webster says: *Fear is an unpleasant, often strong emotion caused by expectation or awareness of danger. Anxious concern; panic, terror, alarmed, frightened or trepidation.*

Roget's says: *Fear is nervousness, care, apprehension, mistrust, timorousness, consternation, phobia, dismay, disquietude, and hesitation.*

Bernanos says: *Fear is a savage frenzy of all insanities of which we are capable.*

Jesus Christ says: "I have not given you the spirit of fear; but of power, and of love, and of a sound mind." (II Timothy 1:7)

What fears are you allowing to hold you back? What fears are you allowing to torment you? What fears are you nursing? What fears are you trying to get over? What fears are you using as an excuse? What fears are you allowing to suffocate your dreams? What fears have a grip on your life? What fears do you allow to minimize your self-worth? What fears are deep within you? What fears do you pretend not to have? What fears have kept you from Millionaire status? What fears have kept you in debt all of your life? What fears have caused you stress? What fears have caused you anxiety? What fears are you allowing to control your inner most thoughts, desires and possibilities for your life?

Tally up your fears
(because it's time to get rid of them)

_____

_____

_____

_____

_____

_____

_____

_____

_____

Behavior therapists, psychologists and social workers will tell you that fear is a natural occurrence when man is faced with an issue. This is true because everyone is fearful of something. The secret to dealing with your fear is in the way you respond and relate to it. I wanted you to make a list because you need to see for yourself how ridiculous it is to be afraid of what you wrote down. Fear is nothing but what you make it. It has no special power except the power you give it. Consider it to be a shadow on the ground that follows you around and waits for you to react to it. The strange thing is that you can't touch it, smell it or taste it, but you can always recognize its affects.

A wise man once said, "There's nothing to fear, but fear itself." Besides, you read that God Almighty has not given us the spirit of fear, but He has provided us with a sound mind, meaning our mind is the battleground for how we attack, dismantle, shrink down or use fear to our advantage. I believe that every man should do like the one book says, "Feel the fear and do it any way." Don't allow fear to stop you. Accept the fact that you are afraid and go on anyway to whatever dream, destiny or goal you may have.

For years, I was afraid to ride a motorcycle and I knew in my mind that it was legitimate to have a fear of a machine that could take my life in a split second. So you know what I did? I took motorcycle lessons to improve myself in the area of riding a motorcycle. Why would I be a fool and jump on a Harley Davidson and ride down a busy intersection untrained? Not me! I'm a little smarter than that. This is what I'm urging you to do, Top Achiever. If you have a fear of something, meet it head on and allow it to fuel the fire within to get the proper training, so you can come back and kick fear in the butt.

Don't Doubt Your Power

*"The only thing that is
consistent in this world is
life and death. Everything
else is subject to chance."*
— Anonymous

What does doubt do to an individual? It creates a level of uncertainty that causes distraction from the original plans, dreams and purpose. One thing that seems to happen to a lot of people is that before they can make the commitment, they want to be 100% certain that the idea, plan, format, goal and dream is going to work for them. Instead of realizing that they have already shown up with the power, talent and the gifts needed, they slow their progress by doubting their own God-given abilities. Have you ever prepared for something and right before it was time to execute it, you began to doubt yourself? Or have you ever been around someone who was doing something you liked and you could actually do it better, but you doubted yourself when it came time to perform? Can doubt be cured? Yes. Allow me to administer an inoculate for doubt: ACTION. Action will bring forth the very death of fear and doubt. Getting involved and becoming an active participant in your future removes doubt. While you're in action, you don't have time to doubt yourself. Why? Because you're too busy taking care of business to doubt. The power within you is more powerful than anything. Remember, you are a unique person with great vision and ability and I doubt you would deny that. Let me give you a few examples of a few non-doubters who believed in the power of their dreams so strongly that it drove them far beyond Doubtersville.

- **Amy Scherber, 37,** didn't doubt and took a risk to

open a bread bakery in New York City. She prepared her own signature creations of different breads and now she provides baked goods to over 30 different stores throughout New York City. Speaking of bread, she's earned a lot of it, over **$3 Million** in sales last year.

- **JoAnne Jonathan, 39,** didn't doubt that she wanted to open up her own clinic in an industry that's heavily dominated by men. While still working as a physical therapist, she devised a plan to provide special needs to blue-collar workers and last year she cracked and massaged over **$7 Million.**

- **Randy Wachtler, 39,** didn't doubt, although he started his business in a very unusual place. He started out smack-dab in the middle of a Nashville radio station producing commercial jingles and catchy themes. He now whistles to the tune of over **$2 Million** for his services.

- **Jerry Yang, 33,** didn't doubt his dream of starting his own computer company and became the co-founder of Yahoo. Now he's yahooooing to a tune of **$570 Million.**

- **Michael Dell, 37,** didn't doubt. He started thinking of having his own computer to market and sell as he sat in his University of Texas dorm room. Now he's worth over **$11 Billion.** That's right ... **Billion Dollars!**

CHAPTER SEVEN

Begin to Think and
Act Like a
MILLIONAIRE

Begin To Think And Act Like A MILLIONAIRE

"The man who will use his skill and
constructive imagination to see how
much he can give for a dollar, instead
of how little he can give for a dollar
is bound to succeed."
— Henry Ford

The most common misconception about men and women who have used their skills, talents and courage to accumulate wealth is that they're not like you and me. We automatically assume that because they have achieved a certain level of wealth that somehow they have become better than us. We don't know why, we just do. It has become a natural phenomenon to be overly impressed with someone because of his or her wealth. We feel that they are smarter than us and they have some special power within themselves that we don't have.

As part of our society, we have become consumed with the idea that wealthy people are from an entirely different planet and they are to be looked upon as alien lifeforms that are graciously paying us a visit here on Planet Earth. Or we go to the other end of the spectrum and say that they're just extremely lucky individuals. I don't know how many times someone has said to me, "You sure are lucky to be doing what you're doing. I wish I had luck like you. Come over here and let me rub you for luck." That really makes me laugh because it wasn't luck that helped me accumulate wealth. It was through a lot of prayer, hard work, sacrifice and a little elbow grease. A wise man once said, "Luck is for people who don't prepare, so if you're prepared you don't need luck." Another common belief is that Millionaires, especially young Millionaires, are spoiled little brats who were born with a silver spoon in their mouth and somehow their mommies and daddies just took them by the hand and sat a cool Million dollars in their lap to play with.

Trust me, it doesn't happen as often as you think. I have a really good friend whose dad owns a thriving car dealership. His dealership is one of the top Black-owned businesses in the country. It has been owned and operated by her dad for over 30 years. Last year alone, the dealership earned over $200 Million in sales and leasing. Would you find it striking to believe that my friend still has to pay her own car note lease and insurance? That's right, she still pays like everyone else. She's daddy's little girl but she's also daddy's little consumer. The only thing extra special that daddy's big bucks has done for her was paid her entire education expenses to law school, which included every book, every class, tuition, allowance, $2,000 a month rent, groceries and provided her with a brand new Mustang to get back and forth to class. After that he was finished. He felt that he had prepared her for success and it was now up to her to choose to go down the path. My good friend went on to complete law school at the top of her class, but she's still not a Millionaire. She works at daddy's dealership in the used car section and deals with bills, stress and anxiety, just like most individuals.

This type of thinking is dangerous because of the limitations that we place on ourselves. If you believe that someone is better than you because they have more money than you, it's a high possibility that you will allow a person's wealth to minimize your goals, dreams and commitment. A person is not wealth and wealth is not a person. If someone creates a path for himself or herself and it brings about wealth in their life, it doesn't mean that they have more value than you do. It simply means that they have a little more training than you. Money doesn't make the person, the person makes the money. Millionaires are just common folks who have mastered the art of accumulating wealth. Yes, there is magic in the power of genius but there is no magic involved in accumulating wealth.

Remember that most Millionaires are just like you and me. I'll prove it! We all have two eyes, a pair of lips, a mouth, ears, teeth, arms, legs, feet, a spirit and the power of God and all of his greatness inside of us. The most fascinating thing I discovered about my captain, a man of great wealth and affluence, is that he puts his pants on one leg at a time just like I do. He cries like me, he smiles like me, he has joy like me, he has pain like me, he loves like me, he enjoys life like me, he has bad days like me, and the only major difference that I found was that **he doesn't spend like me because he's got a lot more money than me.** Everything else was the same! Be grateful in the fact that these people have unlocked the mystery to wealth and abundance. If they can do it, so can you.

MILLIONAIRES and Academics

"Success is that old ABC ...
Ability, Breaks and Courage."
— Charles Luckman

Did you know that on the Forbes list of the 400 richest people in America at least 131 of the members never graduated from college? But combined they have more wealth than China, Great Britain and France. Here's another shocking fact to consider: If you interviewed the average Millionaire, you would find that they were not considered to be one of the smartest kids in grammar school, high school or college. The average Millionaires' grade point average during their high school and college career was a 2.6. Most Millionaires will even tell you that they got all C's in high school and never enjoyed a minute of it. Some Millionaires will also tell you that they had learning disabilities growing up, they were held back a grade, they flunked their ACTs, law school rejected them, they received D's and F's in classes like history, English and handwriting.

They may even tell you that their behavior was terrible, they couldn't stay focused or they come from a bad household. You may even hear that they flunked out of school, left home at a young age, that they were terrible in geometry and calculus. You may hear that they come from a single parent home that didn't promote education. You may hear that they were ranked at the bottom of their class during graduation. You may even hear that school was a joke to them and they only attended because they were forced to. Well, how is it that they are so inadequate and they have managed to become filthy rich?

I thought Millionaires were these super intelligent life forms who got all A's in school, sang in the choir and wore white short sleeve dress shirts, checkered pants and prescription glasses. **WRONG!!!**

Now that may be true for some Millionaires but not all Millionaires. There are a lot of Billionaires and Millionaires that were average students with average grades and beyond average bank accounts. You do not have to be a rocket scientist, astrophysicist or a person with a perfect IQ. What you do have to have is a heart, courage, backbone and tenacity.

So what:
- You failed your college entrance exam.
- You were a slow reader.
- You got all C's in school.
- You are not as fast as others in mathematics.
- You failed a class in the 10th grade.
- You couldn't spell.
- You flunked out of college.
- Your grade point average was below a 2.0.
- Your classmates were smarter than you.
- You have a General Education Degree.
- You stutter.
- You couldn't see the board in school, so your grades were low.
- Your LSAT score kept you out of law school.
- Your MCAT score wasn't high enough for medical school.
- Your GRE score didn't meet the requirement for graduate school.

The only thing you should be concerned with is **WHAT ARE YOU GOING TO DO ABOUT IT?**

There are three types of people in the world: People who make things happen, people who watch things happen, and people who say WHAT HAPPENED?

Which one are you? Are you the type to make things happen? If so, forget about your educational past and focus in on making something happen today. Then once you accumulate your Millions, people will call you a genius.

How Does A MILLIONAIRE Define Success?

"Wealth is not in making money, but in making the man while he is making money."
— John Wicker

Most Millionaires will tell you that success to them is finding complete and total enjoyment in what they do. Some will also tell you that success means that they are able to provide for their families. Then you will have some say that success is "the new person I have become as a result of having the courage to live my dreams, experience life and see my vision manifest itself." Most of us believe that success is making a lot of money, buying big homes, driving fancy cars, taking long trips and being recognized in public. Yes, all of those things come with being successful but they are not the most important things to consider. As I conducted my interviews with Millionaires for my research, I encountered several interesting people who have their own testimony of what success means to them.

The first gentleman I interviewed was a former juvenile delinquent runaway, a former substance abuser and a violent criminal who had been arrested five times before he was 16-years-old. He is now a young Millionaire with a thriving sanitation company that removes trash from office buildings, restaurants and communities. I asked him, "What does success mean to you? He replied, "Success to me means being able to be an example to another young person of what not to do and how to correct it."

I interviewed a young lady who was molested and raped by her mother's boyfriend for 11 consecutive years, homeless at one point in her life, and addicted to crack as a baby. Now she's a young 38-year-old Millionaire with real estate all over the Midwest. I asked her, "How do you define success?" She responded, "Success to me is being able to be able to give back to my community and provide counseling and funding to shelters for girls."

I interviewed another young lady who was kidnapped as a little girl and raised in a foster home until she was 16. She is now a young Millionaire who designs and creates websites for large corporations. I asked her to define success. She said, "I would define success as a tool to help someone else who is less fortunate than me. God has blessed me tremendously and He has made me to be a blessing to many."

The last gentleman I interviewed was a high school drop out in the 10th grade with a tremendous self-esteem problem because he was burned on over 80% of his body when he was 9-years-old and his mother kept him in the basement for a number of years afterwards. He is now a 41-year-old young Millionaire who now runs his own computer software company that provides training for large corporations. When asked, "How would you define success?" He said, "I feel that success is having the courage to look inside yourself and realize that you are great despite your outer appearance. If a person is able to do that, then they are successful."

A MILLIONAIRE'S Thought Process

*"I know the price of success: dedication,
hard work and an unremitting devotion
to the things you want to see happen."*
— Frank Lloyd Wright

One of the most common denominators that Millionaires share is not the fact that they have Millions of dollars. It is the fact that they possess a tremendous amount of courage and tenacity. Any Millionaire alive will tell you that without courage and tenacity you will be eaten up alive. Unfortunately, we can't go online and click to purchase a double order of courage and several months worth of tenacity. Courage is something that has to come from inside and has been developed over a period of time. Courage is not something that you master overnight. Courage is developed through life experiences, failures, defeats, setbacks and disappointments. In order for you to be able to build up your courage, you have to be willing to take a chance on failing. That's one of the major keys to developing a Millionaire thought process. A poet once wrote, "If you're not willing to risk, you're not willing to grow, and if you're not willing to grow, you're not willing to be happy, and if you're not willing to be happy, then what else is there?"

Develop your courage and become a risk taker. What's the worst thing that can happen? You strike out and lose the game. So what? Did you know in baseball if you have a .333 percentage batting average that you're considered to be one of the top hitters in the world and you can make it to the Hall of Fame? That's a 1 in 3 chance of you hitting a little white ball. Are you afraid that you might make a mistake? Did you know that the average Top Achiever and Millionaire makes over 10,000 mistakes a month?

Do you feel that if you try, people might think that you

are crazy? Did you know that his own family committed J.C. Penney to a psychiatric hospital because he wanted to open department stores all over the country? Then before he died, he was worth well over **$2 Billion**.

Are you afraid of risking a little money on yourself? Did you know that Walt Disney went bankrupt seven times before he landed his first television show? Now Disney Productions does hundreds of Millions of revenue each year. Are you afraid that your dream may take too long? Kobe Bryant came out of high school and went on to be the youngest NBA player in history to win three championships. Are you afraid that you're not smart enough? Read about this guy — he may sound familiar to you. At age 4, he could barely talk. As he grew up, he could not read or write. He flunked out of high school, failed his college entrance exam twice and, at age 24, he had a lonely job as an office assistant but he had a tremendous amount of courage. Who was he? Albert Einstein, one of the most intelligent men in scientific history.

Webster says tenacity is: *being attentive and not easily pulled apart; holding fast and being tough.*

Roget's says tenacity is: *strength, stick-to-itiveness, and perseverance, unyielding, unwavering, persistent and steadfast.*

Millionaires say: *Doing whatever it takes to get the job done even if you are outmatched, outgunned and out of money. **The way you win is to go after your dream like you're out of your mind.***

Having tenacity to go after your dream and all the wealth that you believe that you deserve is going to take a lot of energy and tough skin. I can tell you right now, if you were to ask 500 people to help you accomplish your goal, only 2% would actually take the time to help you. Top Achiever, that means one thing, you have to be prepared to hear the word **NO!** Get used to it now if you plan to be a Millionaire! I guarantee that you will be told **NO** 50 times more than you hear the word YES as you travel down the long road of achieving maximum success for your life. Why? I don't know. That's just the way it is and it's called **life.** Life is not made to bring you up. It's made to bring you down. What's the law of gravity that governs our universe? "What goes up must come down." Now let me give you the secret to developing your tenacity and not allowing life to bring you down. Use the answer **NO** as a vitamin to re-energize you. Allow the word NO to boost your spirit. This may sound like a difficult concept to swallow because we have been mentally conditioned to accept the answer NO as a negative. When we allow the negative effects to creep into our spirits, it dismantles our dreams and kills our opportunities. If you use NO as a vitamin and allow it to energize you, it will give you the tenacity that you need to hold fast to your dreams, goals, ambitions and desires.

A few years ago, when I decided to go after my dream of becoming an administrator in the Detroit Public Schools, life came to pay me a visit. I went on interview after interview and each time the panel found a reason to bypass me and tell me NO. This only fueled my fire to prove that I could do it. A few months later, I went on another three interviews and every one of them told me NO. A couple months before it was time to dismiss school for the year, I interviewed with two other schools. Once again, I was told NO. I could see the look of pleasure in their eyes as they told me. It seemed as though they were telling me in slow motion, like in the movie "The Matrix," NOOOOOOOOO.

Now, I did experience a feeling of disappointment, but I wasn't finished. In my mind, the deal was not done until somebody told me YES. In September of 2000, a few weeks after my birthday, I received a phone call to interview with a school that had 1,100 elementary children, the highest enrollment in Michigan. I didn't care. I wanted a yes and I wasn't moved by the size or girth of the school. My interview went well and everyone was impressed with me except one woman who seemed like a demon straight from hell. She looked at me and said, "Mr. Edison, given your lack of experience, your lack of knowledge, your lack of training, your lack of age, your lack of exposure, your lack of curriculum knowledge, and your lack of time spent in education, what makes you believe that you can perform such a huge task of being an assistant principal at the largest school in Michigan?" The panel of 15 was frozen and all eyes were shifted on me. My answer depended upon my tenacity and courage that I had within myself. I sat up in the chair, cleared my throat, and said, "Because it's simple ... I have the capacity to read and comprehend." Now that may sound cocky but it's not. It's exuding courage to prove that I am who I say I am. Did you know that if you looked up the word *cocky* you wouldn't find a definition? What you will find is that it will refer you to *pert* and *pert* will refer you to *confident*. Be pert, be courageous and for God's sake, man, have some tenacity.

"He who is not courageous enough
to take risks
will accomplish nothing
in life."
— The Greatest,
Muhammad ALI

Attributes of a MILLIONAIRE

"In the last analysis, our only
freedom is the freedom
to discipline ourselves."
— Bernard Baruch

A self-made Millionaire that has evolved from poverty to prominence picks up beneficial habits and develops certain characteristics along the way. Which means that he or she can be identified by the quality of work and by the way in which they operate. I want you to take the

"Who wants to be a Millionaire"
Characteristic Challenge.

Directions: If you have the characteristic, write the letters **IHA** next to the choice, which means *I have it already*. If you don't have it, write letters **IDH**, which means *I don't have it*. Now, if you slightly have it but not completely, write the letters **IND** which means *I need development*.

These are the top 20 characteristics of a Millionaire
in no particular order.

1. **Millionaires have strong religious faith in God** _____
2. **Millionaires are very well disciplined**_____
3. **Millionaires are very supportive**_____
4. **Millionaires work harder than most people**_____
5. **Millionaires have a very competitive nature and spirit** _____
6. **Millionaires are very well organized** _____
7. **Millionaires live below their means** _____
8. **Millionaires are very honest with people** _____
9. **Millionaires have strong leadership ability** _____
10. **Millionaires look for solutions instead of problems** _____
11. **Millionaires have great personalities**_____
12. **Millionaires possess integrity** _____

13. Millionaires have self-control over spending _____
14. Millionaires read more than the average person ____
15. Millionaires invest more than $5,000 a year into their own personal professional development _____
16. Millionaires have the urge to be well respected ____
17. Millionaires are excellent time managers _____
18. Millionaires know their weaknesses _____
19. Millionaires are highly supportive of their spouses_____
20. Millionaires are family oriented _____

Now, if you don't fit the description of a Millionaire, don't feel bad. What you do now is begin to develop yourself, so you will. It's a process that takes time and you must not rush it. Think of it as a brand new baby being conceived. God designates nine months to create, mold and cultivate one of the world's greatest events, the birth of a newborn baby. God never rushes the process He always takes His time.

"To everything there is a season, and a time to every purpose under the heaven."
Eccl 3:1

Who Do MILLIONAIRES Listen To?

*"Wherefore my beloved brethren,
let every man be swift to hear,
slow to speak and slow to wrath."*
— James 1:19

In the face of unpopular belief, many Millionaires and extremely prosperous people will tell you that they seek to hear from God first. Nearly every young Millionaire I interviewed proclaimed God as the reason for their success. Therefore, who better to take advice from? If God is the one who provides the wind, the waves, the trees, the protection, the finances, the opportunity, the love, the gifts, the wisdom, the favor, the grace, the mercy, the healing power, the drive, the energy, the courage, the sun, the moon, the stars, the currency, the ability, the health, the means, the internet, the economy, the planet, the air, the food, the home, the appointment, the fax machine, the contact, the confidence, the faith, the elements, the support, the nerves, the guts, the fearlessness, the growth, the presentation and the Million Dollar abundance train that runs you over,

WHO ELSE WOULD YOU LISTEN TO?

Top Achiever, it's simple. If you do not communicate with God on a daily basis, you are not going to be able to hear the good things that He has to offer you. Of course, Millionaires listen to stockbrokers, market analysts, reporters, CPAs, business partners, stock reports, tax specialists, insurance agents, the spouse, investment managers, relatives, lending institutions, real estate agents, life insurance agents, colleagues, friends, bank presidents and even the dog, sometimes. All of those people are great and probably good at what they do. BUT **GOD** IS SO MUCH BETTER!!

The bible says, ***"Seek ye first the kingdom of God, and his***

righteousness; and all these things shall be added unto you."
— Matt. 6:33

How Do MILLIONAIRES Live?

*"Always strive to get on the top
in life because it's the bottom
that's overcrowded."*
— Anonymous

During my research, I found that most Millionaires are married and have an average of three kids with a divorce rate of 4%. Although there is an increasing amount of young hot, single Millionaires on the market, the older generation of Millionaires have families and nice safe homes. Of the average Millionaires who do have families, 50% of the wives do not work outside the home. They are usually into some type of sales or marketing that can be done from the home, which enables the wife to spend more time with the kids. This is not to say that all women should stay at home barefoot and pregnant. I'm simply giving you statistics, so give me a break! I love working, successful, sharp, strong, direct, energetic, confident, self-assured, smart, genius-like, beautiful, kind, loving and bringing home the bacon-type women.

Here's a few more statistics that may shock you:
- **Almost all Millionaires buy their household products in bulk.**
- **Some Millionaires, to save money, have their shoes resoled.**
- **Some Millionaires drive cars that are more than ten years old.**
- **Most Millionaires spend a minimum of $1,000 on books.**
- **Nearly all Millionaires wait for things to go on sale.**
- **Very few Millionaires buy brand new homes.**
- **Most Millionaires live off their investments.**
- **Most Millionaires never purchase wedding rings**

over $4,000.

- Most Millionaires find it preposterous to spend over $100,000 on a car.
- Most Millionaires don't loan money to family members.
- Some Millionaires mow their own lawns.
- Some Millionaires would never spend over $50 for a hairdo.
- Almost all Millionaires look for bargains.
- Almost all Millionaires spend less than $3,000 at the mall each year.
- A lot of new Millionaires prefer to cook rather than have carry out.
- Most Millionaires invest in more that one stock.
- Almost every Millionaire loves to be frugal.
- Very few Millionaires shop in the name of "I deserve it."
- Mostly all Millionaires participate in hobbies that soothe them.
- Some Millionaires believe that cable television is a waste of money.
- Most Millionaires allow their children to attend public school.
- Very few Millionaires purchase homes worth over a Million Dollars.
- Almost all Millionaires pay their credit cards on time.
- The majority of Millionaires operate on a cash basis only.
- A great number of Millionaires enjoy being regular people with a large bank account.

These statistics are pretty shocking after the last decade of Bling-Bling that we have watched on MTV and BET. I thought all Millionaires drove half Million-dollar cars, wore Millions of dollars in diamonds and had homes the size of football stadiums. **NOT TRUE!** Allow me to let you in on a little secret. The Bling-Bling, the big diamonds, the mink coats, the furs, the Bentleys, the Hummers, the private jets and all of the finer things in life that come across the screen in rap videos are

RENTED, LEASED AND MUST GO BACK!

How Is A MILLIONAIRE Productive?

*"The ability to concentrate and to
use your time well is everything."*
— Lee Iacocca

How is your focus, concentration and planning? Are you easily distracted away from your goals? Do you lack the ability to concentrate? Are you an effective planner? If not, you are missing three vital components of being a successful Millionaire. The average Millionaire will tell you that the ability to concentrate is very, very valuable. I remember when I played Little League basketball. My concentration was horrible. Every time I would get up to the free throw line, I would brick both shots, no matter what I did. I tried to take my time and shoot but the crowd wouldn't stop yelling. I tried the breathing technique the coach recommended, but as soon as I got up to the free throw line, I still bricked both shots.

The reason my concentration was off was because subconsciously I really didn't want to make the free throws. I just wanted to play in the game. Consciously, I thought about making the free throws, but deep inside me, I refused to put forth the mental energy it required to keep me cool under pressure. Did you know that concentration is nothing but giving your attention to a single thing or object? If you plan to reach your goals, conquer your fears and live out your dreams. You're going to have to pay attention to the one single thing that's most important to you. I was watching the Masters Golf Tournament, which showed a closeup of Tiger Woods as he was going for the winning putt. He was concentrating so hard that he almost pushed the ball in with his thoughts. After he won the tournament, the announcer went

166

over to Tiger and asked, "Tiger, how were you able to make that incredible putt with Millions of people's eyes watching you?" He responded, "Because I don't enjoy losing. It doesn't matter how many people are watching, 1 or 100 Million. I plant my feet and my concentration takes care of the rest."

Are You A Good Planner?

*"What you have to do and the
way you have to do it is incredibly simple.
Whether you are willing to
do it, that's another matter."*
— Peter Drucker

I was attending a church service a few years ago and we had a guest pastor by the name of T.D. Jakes. He said something that almost caused me to slide up under my seat from a strong feeling of conviction. He said," I want you to take a look at your life right now. Who you are and the things that you have is a direct result of your willingness to pray and to plan. So stop complaining to God about what you don't have and starting leading your life by planning it, directing it and being progressive instead of digressive. Plan your life now, today, before someone else plans it for you." Wow! And I thought I was broke because God wasn't answering my prayers. From that day forward, I planned everything I did down to the half hour. Breakfast, lunch, dinner, school, work, church, sports, shopping, reading, writing, travel time, money and anything else impeding my progress as a successful individual.

You've heard the old saying, "If you fail to plan, you plan to fail." That quote is so simple and about a hundred years old, but it still stands true in life today. If you don't plan, you will find yourself being led by life, instead of you leading it. Do you realize the amount time you waste from not planning? Not to mention the amount of money you can lose. I used to be Mr. Last Minute Everything. I did everything just in the nick of time. I never planned and I never planned on planning. Until one year, Mr. You Know Who caught up with me and cost me big time. At the last minute, I decided that I wanted to attend a Stevie Wonder concert.

I called a friend of mine and asked her if she wanted to go. She said yes, but it was going to be at least an hour before she could be ready. It was 7:00 p.m. then and the concert began at 7:30 p.m. I picked her up right around 8:15 p.m. and we were on our way to the theatre. Once we arrived, I discovered that all of the parking lots were filled and I had to park on the street. When we got to the ticket window, the only tickets available cost $125 a piece. As soon as we took our seats, I realized that Stevie was finishing up his last 15 minutes of his set. Frustrated and irate, my date and I left the theatre to go have dinner. Surprise! No dinner! The car was gone! Apparently, I had parked in a no parking zone and the police towed my car away. The only thing I can remember saying is, "Why me? Why me? Why me? Why me? Why? Why? Why? Why? Why?" Then life answered back with *Why not you? Who would you suggest?*

Top Achiever, planning is the key for complete and total success. Come on and try it! All the Millionaires are doing it!

Start Planning Now!

MILLIONAIRE PLANNER
Day 1

ACTIVITIES   TIMES

1. _____

2. _____

3. _____

4. _____

5. _____

6. _____

7. _____

8. _____

9. _____

10. _____

Reflection: _____

_____

Go online today and order your very own *"Millionaire Planner"* at **www.jonathanedisonspeaks.com**

CHAPTER EIGHT

*Avoid Negative People
and Circumstances*

Avoid Negative People and Negative Circumstances

"Do not lose your inward peace for
anything whatsoever, even if your
whole world seems upset."
— Saint Frances de Sales

Growing up as a kid in the ghetto in Detroit, Michigan, I soon realized that negative people and circumstances were as common as Popsicles and Pro-Keds. I watched as young kids my age became influenced by the negative people around them and wound up serving time in a federal penitentiary or in Swanson's Funeral Home. I grew up in a neighborhood where it was easy to run into a tough situation and even easier to be led into one. I remember when I was 15-years-old, every young kid in my neighborhood wanted to be Tony Montana, who played in the movie "Scarface," king of the underworld. The young guys dreamed about dealing drugs, dressing nice, making money and having the most beautiful women you've ever laid eyes on. At the time, I knew a lot of people who sold drugs, but I was no criminal. I was a coward. That's right, scared to go to jail. Scared to have "Big Bubba" on my little booty.

I had a really good friend by the name of Patrick who was hell bent on being a gangster. One day I was on my way to work and Patrick pulled up in a white Ford station wagon and told me to get in; he would take me to work. Now I knew Patrick didn't have a job and he loved stealing cars, but I wanted to ride in a car rather than on the bus. So he drove me to work and, of course, the car was stolen. The funny thing was that he was driving it like it belonged to him. Patrick was leaning to the side with the radio blasting and all of the windows down without a care in the world. After he dropped me off, I swore never to get in a stolen car again as long as I lived.

Wouldn't you know it? Patrick came by my house again two weeks later, only this time he was driving a stolen Bonneville and he had big dreams of making money on the brain. Patrick jumped out of the car and reached into his right hand pants pocket and pulled out $3,000 worth of uncut crack cocaine. I was shocked and fascinated all at the same time. Patrick stuffed it back in his pocket and told me about a plan for us to get rich. My first mind and my gut feeling told me to just walk away, but I couldn't. It looked too good and too easy for me to pass up a chance to make $1,500 cash money. Patrick's plan was to drive the stolen Bonneville to a neighborhood, park it, and walk ten blocks over to known drug addicts that needed drugs. I told him, "No problem. Let's do it. I'm ready to get paid."

After driving around for about an hour, we found a place to park the Bonneville and set up shop to start making money. We parked in front of a white house that sat on the corner of a four way intersection. We had everything planned and we were ready to get out of the car. Suddenly, Patrick started burning rubber in front of the house. I mean really burning rubber. He had his foot on the brake and he had the gas pedal to the floor. This knucklehead burned rubber for so long that it caused a huge cloud of smoke to rise up and cover the entire four way intersection. I jumped out of the car and started laughing so hard I almost wet my pants.

My laughter was brought to an abrupt halt once the smoke cleared. After we had a great big laugh, we decided to walk over to sell the crack. As the smoke cleared, sitting on the other side of the street were two police cars with their lights turned off. I looked at Patrick and he looked at me. I said, "Which way are you going to run, because I don't want to run over you?" He pointed left and I took off running to the right. Those police officers were pissed. They couldn't believe we ran from them. They came after us in hot pursuit. As a matter of a fact they called in several other police officers for reinforcement. Patrick and I ran for hours, trying to avoid prison. I remember sliding up under a pickup truck to hide out and catch my breath. As I lay on the cold, oily concrete, I kept thinking how stupid I was to let him talk me into this. Luckily, back then, I was a lot faster than I am now. Had I avoided negative people and negative circumstances, I wouldn't have ended up in a negative situation.

Get Out Of Their Way

*"Some people can't stand it
when other people go after it."*
— Jonathan Edison

Have you ever been on the road driving along and some maniac comes barreling down the road doing about 100 m.p.h. and forces you to run off the road just to avoid being killed? If yes, I hope it doesn't happen to you again. If no, be on the lookout. Here's the question: why did you pull over? The obvious answer is you didn't want to be killed. Look at it this way: you pulled over so you could avoid danger, destruction, possible injuries and an accident, which may have led to your death.

Top Achiever, allow me to forewarn you, as you drive down the road of success, you will experience not one but multiple maniacs who are trying to destroy, destruct and cause you to have an accident and kill your dream. I like to call these people PLAYER HATERS. It's very bewildering to me that when individuals decide to get in the game of life, you will have PLAYER HATERS out there waiting to try to sabotage a player's game. They will try everything to get you to lose focus and veer off the road. I remember my first day on the job as the new assistant principal of K.B. White Elementary School. I was so happy that I couldn't stop grinning. I was speaking to everyone and I was trying to be really friendly. Then the PLAYER HATERS broke out of their huddle and came after me. I had someone who stopped me in the hallway and asked, "Don't you think you're too young for this job?" I had another person stop me and say, "Your crazy for taking this job." Another person stopped me and said, "I've never worked for a young man before. I think my son is your age."

I was outdone because I thought everyone was as happy

as I was about my new job. Then I had the ultimate happen. This older teacher, who shall remain nameless, came into my office, looked me in the face and said, "Son, I hope you don't think you're going to be bossing me around because I have underwear that are older than you." I smiled and said, "Well, don't you think it's about time you got some new ones." I walked away and went on about my business. Why were these people PLAYER HATING me? I don't know and I don't care. I just know that the more successful you become, the more PLAYER HATERS are going to come barreling down your road. Top Achiever, always remember PLAYER HATERS are like bad drivers — you just have to get out of their way.

Give Up Power To Achieve Victory

*"A man having an argument
by himself is considered to be crazy."*
— Anonymous

Why do we entertain fools? Have you ever tried to argue somebody down just to make a point? You had to get the last word in and you had to let them know who you were. You had to prove your point and after exerting all of that unnecessary energy, you still weren't any closer to a solution than when you began. All you had to do was stop arguing with them. I know! That's not the point. You have to be right all the time and if someone disagrees with you, look out! You're going to give them a piece of your mind. Understand that Millionaires do not have this type of attitude. A Millionaire's stance is that he or she will give up temporary power to achieve victory.

I remember as I was driving along, minding my own business in my new Mercedes, a Michigan State Trooper got behind me and pulled me over for no reason at all. I was driving the appropriate speed limit, I had on my seat belt, all of my lights were working properly and my tags on my car were up to date. I wondered why he was pulling me over. I immediately became irritated. I pulled the car over and the trooper got out of his car and came up to my window. I was ready to let him have it. I felt that he was pulling me over for no apparent reason and I wasn't going to stand for it. I rolled down my window and demanded an explanation. The trooper yelled back and told me that if I didn't calm down that he was going to have to arrest me.

Now I had a choice. I could give up temporary power and achieve victory without receiving a ticket, or I could continue to argue and possibly receive a ticket and a night in "happy land." Luckily for me, my brain was working prop erly that day. As the trooper got louder, I started to whisper. Then he got even louder and before I knew it, he was arguing with himself because I had already given up the power to achieve the victory. By the way, I didn't go to jail, but he still gave me a ticket.

People Are Going To Be People

"When someone throws you a hot potato,
you don't have to catch it."
— Jonathan Edison

That's right, don't catch it! Understand that people aren't going to like you for a number of reasons and it's okay. What you have to be careful of is not to entertain the negative thoughts or hot potatoes that people are going to throw at you. You know why I call them hot potatoes? Because these are the comments that burn you up inside. They cause you to think irrationally, emotionally and even violently. Has anyone ever made a terrible comment to you? Then you drove home as fast as you could and immediately got on the phone to call everyone that you knew and tell them you couldn't believe this person had said such a horrible thing to you?

Have you ever been sitting around with a group of friends and one of your friends made a comment to you in fun but it really hurt your feelings? Have you ever been told that you were ugly? Have you ever been told you were going to be a failure? Have you ever been told that you were worthless? Have you ever been told that you were stupid? Have you ever been told that you were insignificant? Have you ever been told that you would never amount to anything? If you answered yes to any of these questions, FANTASTIC!! You know what that means. It means that you have a group of people out there who care enough to make an assessment, complete an evaluation and give you some feedback about how they feel about "themselves," so tell them "thank you" for their comments and then you move on and go about doing your business of changing the world.

179

Top Achiever, get to a point in your life where you realize that people are going to be people and there's nothing that you can do about it. If you don't believe me, ask Jesus, the Son of God. They even talked about Him.

Kill Your Enemies With Kindness

*"A man laughing with honey in his mouth
finds it difficult to be evil and irate."*
— Jonathan Edison

Every man or woman in history who has achieved prominence or anything great has experienced the threat of a tough
enemy or foe. To what degree will you allow this enemy to
get into your camp and cause havoc is completely up to you.
Understand that most of the enemies that will come up
against you aren't really mad at you. They just need help
developing their dream. The reason they have become your
enemy in the first place is because they are underdeveloped,
underachieved and they are looking for someone that they
can bring down to their level. I had a situation once where I
was selected to be the principal of a summer school academy
and the lead teacher, for no reason at all, began to treat me
like an enemy.

I didn't understand because I was just going to be there
for the summer, which was about five weeks. To this teacher,
the length of time was irrelevant. He persisted on being a
spiteful and nasty person towards me. I tried to speak to him
and that didn't work. I tried to joke with him and that didn't
work. I even tried to be interested in what he was interested
in and that didn't work either. I didn't know what other
method of leadership to try until I remembered an old trick
that a principal taught me years ago. The principal told me
that anytime he had to deliver bad news to the staff, he
would always provide doughnuts, coffee and juice in the
morning. He said, "If they were upset or angry with him,
they quickly forgot when they saw the free food." So I tried
it.

The very next day, I brought in a couple dozen Krispy
Krème doughnuts and orange juice to see what type of

181

response I would receive. I couldn't believe it. The same guy who appeared to be my enemy was standing in my door with cinnamon sugar around his mouth talking about the Lakers game. Kill your enemy with kindness. It's a lot easier than trying to battle with them.

Love The HELL Out Of Them

"Love your enemies, bless them that
curse you, do good to them that hate
you, and pray for them which despitefully
use you, and persecute you."
— Matt. 5:44

As we go through life, evil things, evil spirits and evil people will show up and cause major damage in our lives, damage that will hurt physically, mentally, financially and even spiritually. Statistics have shown that out of all the damage we suffer, more than 60% of the damage caused in your life will be caused by a family member or a close friend. It went on to say that family members are one of the leading causes for some business owners to lose their businesses. The family business starts out fine and then something tragic takes place.

I have a good friend who married into a wealthy family that owned a transportation company. Everything was going great — the business was booming and the profits were rolling in. Her husband, who managed the operation, decided that he wanted to take a vacation with his lovely new bride. So he put his older brother in charge for ten days until he returned. When the couple returned, they were stunned to find out that the brother had sold the family business and moved out of the country.

At times like this in your life, look to God for love, because if you hold on to the pain that anyone causes you, it is impossible for God to bless a mess. A mess is the strife that's in your heart, the anger that's in your soul and the unforgiveness that you hold onto inside of you. The way you handle the tragedy of people who hurt is vital for your growth professionally and spiritually. You will never be able to change and grow professionally if you're not able to change and grow mentally and spiritually. It takes a mentally strong person to handle the pressures of being successful. And it takes a spiritually strong person to be able to love through the pain. The bible says that LOVE conquers all. If someone has bestowed evil unto you, love them anyway. When you do, you give God permission to get involved supernaturally to repair the hurt.

From Me to You
Positive Quotations
For Dealing with Difficult People and Circumstances

*"Sorrow is a fruit. God does
allow it to grown on a branch
that is too weak to bear it."*
— Victor Hugo

*"The will of God will not take
you where the grace of God
cannot keep you."*
— Anon

*"Nothing is so bad that you
have to sit down and go crazy."*
— John Telgen

*"We are troubled on every side,
yet not distressed; we are
perplexed, but not in despair."*
— 2 Cor. 4:8

*"He who can't endure the bad
will never live to see the good."*
— Anon

*"Inside of a ring or out, ain't nothing
wrong with going down. It's staying
down that's wrong.*
— Muhammad Ali

*"For a just man falleth seven times,
and riseth up again."*
— Prov. 24:16

*"When life knocks you down, try and
land on your back because if you can
look up, you can get up."*
— Anon

*"Father give this to me if it's
for my highest good. If not
give me its equivalent or
something better."*
— Anon

*"Be like a steam kettle! Though
it is up to its neck in hot water,
it continues to sing."*
— Anon

*"You're like a tea bag — not much
happens until you've been thrown
in hot water."*
— Anon

"The best way out is through."
— Helen Keller

*"Sin makes its own hell and
goodness its own heaven"*
— Anon

"Tough times don't last,
tough people do."
— Willie Gary

"Every problem has a gift
for you in its hand."
— Richard Bach

"A man can be destroyed
but not defeated."
— Ernest Hemingway

"Things turn out best for people
who make the best of the way
things turn out."
— Art Linkletter

In a battle, every good soldier has survival tactics and, like a good general, I want to equip you with survival tactics of your own.

Here are 20 Survival Tactics to refer to when dealing with difficult people and difficult circumstances.

Survival Tactics 101

1. **Prayer:** If you pray and ask God for assistance in anything, he will assist. God is not moved by tears and He is a gentleman. You have to invite Him in.

2. **Love:** Love is a mighty weapon against the evils in the world. Practice it, embrace it and execute it and watch how it changes your life and circumstances.

3. **Accept their possibility blindness:** Most people who come against you or doubt you really doubt themselves and have low self-esteem and a bad self-image. When they doubt you, they really mean to say, "Please pray for me to get me out of my hell."

4. **Stay cool:** Don't allow circumstances or people to take over your emotions. Being cool is the best thing you can do because trouble doesn't come to stay, it comes to pass.

5. **Help:** Assist or help someone else in trouble and get the focus off yourself. Take some time to stop worrying about your circumstances and you will open the door to get an answer to your problem.

6. **Let them win:** For you it's not worth the stress and aggravation. Choose your battles wisely. Save your energy for the war.

7. **Watch your mouth:** Don't complain, don't murmur don't even whisper how bad your circumstance is. Be careful of what you say because the universe is listening. Your words have power and you can command blessings or you can invite curses.

8. **Deal with circumstances head on:** Leaders lead from the front. If there is a circumstance or person that is causing you discomfort, deal with it directly and immediately. It will save you a lot of pain in the end.

9. **Look for solutions:** Don't rehearse the pain of the circumstance instead of looking for a solution.

10. **Use your power:** You have the power within to deal with any situation. Don't wimp out and forget that you are the powerful and not the powerless.

11. **Excuse yourself:** If you find yourself in an awkward situation with a group of negative people, simply excuse yourself. You have the right to a stress-free life.

12. **Listen up!** Nothing happens until communication takes place. During difficult circumstances, anger and stress can cause you to shut down and lose your focus. Pay close attention to what people are saying around you. It may be helpful.

13. **Don't go:** When things go wrong, don't go with them. Make a decision that you're going to be brave and then commit to it.

14. **Fight your way out:** As people come against you, they will try every trick in the book to knock you down. In the end, it's not how many punches you take but how many you throw back.

15. **Smile:** The power of the smile is underestimated. You can change your entire outlook on your life by just smiling.

16. **Cry:** It's all right to cry sometimes. We're all human. Allow the emotions to flow out of you. Don't allow them to consume you. MEN TOO!

17. **Laugh:** Laughter is good food for the soul. When you laugh at your circumstances, you strip them of

their power.

18. **Rejoice:** Even when difficult people hurt you, rejoice in the pain. Pain causes you to stretch and grow.

19. **Reflect:** When a difficult circumstance arises, you don't have to worry. Reflect back on how good God has been with you in the past and know that He will deliver you out again.

20. **Give thanks:** Thank God that you are still alive!

Take An Inventory Of Your Relationships

"The individuals that you keep company
with are doing one of two things.
They're either raising you up
or they're bringing you down."
— Anon

In life, sometimes the difficult circumstances that are before us are due to unhealthy relationships that we refuse to let go of. It can be an old boyfriend, girlfriend, family member, high school buddy or even the person that you're married to. What I have found out in my own personal life is that in order for me to move forward, I had to get rid of the old baggage. Unhealthy, non-producing relationships cause years of frustration, guilt, pain and discontentment. It's unhealthy for a person to be involved with someone that causes a terrible rush of negative emotions to run through the body. In order for you to grow, stretch and receive all the blessings from God in your life, you have to make a difficult decision. Either you're going to allow that person to continue to hold you back or you're going to go to them and say, "I'm sorry, I'm a new man (or a new woman) and at this junction in my life, I have to do what's best for my inner peace."

Now, I have to warn you. This decision is going to be one of the most difficult things you'll ever do. It will require you to face your fear of losing that individual as a friend, family member, boyfriend, girlfriend, or spouse. That's difficult because we become so dependent on one another that we can't imagine our lives without that person. Just last year, I had to make a difficult decision in my life regarding an unhealthy relationship. I was engaged to a beautiful, kind and sweet woman, but deep inside I knew that I should break it off because we weren't growing together anymore. Our lives were going in two different directions and we were arguing almost every time we came within a few feet of each other.

After months of agonizing over what I should do, I began having really bad chest pains. At first, I blamed them on too much running on the treadmill or too much bench pressing. Then, as time went on, the chest pains became worse and more intense. I went to the doctor to have it checked out but the doctor told me he couldn't find anything wrong with me. He said I was as healthy as a horse and maybe I needed a vacation to ease the stress of work. I didn't need a vacation. I needed to face my fear of letting go of the woman I loved with all of my heart. I needed to move on with my life and allow God to use me, so I could be a blessing to Millions of people with the story of my life.

I finally got up enough courage to tell her and it hurt. I cried before, during and after but I felt so liberated. My soul felt free. My spirit and my new inner man were able to come out. The chest pains stopped after that and I felt so much lighter. For a long time, I was carrying around a huge stack of bricks. But thanks to God, He gave me the courage and wisdom to set the bricks down. Be okay with your decision. You're not telling the person that you don't love them any-more. You're simply saying that you need to take some time to develop yourself. This way, you avoid hard feelings, grudges and broken car windows.

Take an Inventory of Your Relationships.

Make a list of ten people that you come into contact with the most. Then go down the list and one-by-one analyze the relationship. If your energy level goes up when you see them, draw a happy face. If your body feels funny and your heartbeat rises, draw a line through the name. The line means that you need to end that relationship. **NO EXCUSES!!** Trust me, in the end, that unhealthy relationship will save your life and open the door to wealth.

1. _____

2. _____

3. _____

4. _____

5. _____

6. _____

7. _____

8. _____

9. _____

10. _____

Keep Positive People In Your Circle

*"Sometimes you have to believe in
someone else's belief, until
your belief kicks in."*
— Les Brown

Battling to the top of the mountain of success is not an easy task. It's going to require a lot of energy, positive thinking and positive relationships. It is vital on your success journey that you surround yourself with as many successful, positive thinking and speaking people as you can, because on some of your worst days you may need a crutch to lean on. Now if the crutch you lean on is broken down from life and looking for somebody to help them up, what good is the crutch? Now, this doesn't mean that you should call this person every time a little problem arises. It means that you have a support system — a reservoir of positive energy — to draw from if you need a lift.

We all need lifts and encouragement every now and again. It's natural and it's healthy to hear from somebody else that they believe in you. Their belief in you can give you that extra boost to go on and become the greatest _____ *(you fill in the blank)* that this world has ever seen. Surround yourself with positive people and feed off each other's positive energy. Then in a few months, surprise them with an all expense paid trip to Hawaii, because they deserve it after dealing with you.

Stay Out of the Pity-Party

*"Self-pity is a death that has no
resurrection, a sinkhole from
which no rescuing hand can drag."*
— Elizabeth Elliot

Ladies and gentlemen, please rise for the National Pity-Party anthem of wishers, low achievers, onlookers and wussies:

"Nobody knows the trouble I've seen; nobody knows the trouble I've seen."

Top Achiever, I hope and pray that I haven't described you. Understand that we will all have our bad days when we feel like the world and everyone in it is picking on us. We will also go through a period of failure where nothing seems to go right. Then we will have the opportunity to do the tango with Mr. Unforeseen, who comes in and whisks us across the floor. Some of us may be paid a visit by Murphy's Law, who's just waiting for something to go wrong. Every person on the planet who lives and breathes will go through something. But the way to deal with it is not to run to the market and buy a bunch of beverages, chips and dip, put on your best outfit or your prom dress, whichever one still fits, and call all of your friends over for a world famous pity-party. Self-pity is one of the most crippling and consuming defects known to man. It's also a roadblock to all spiritual progress that can cut off all effective communication with God and His blessings. Top Achiever, a pity-party is a party that you cannot afford to crash. When a difficult circumstance arises, don't cry and complain about it. DO SOMETHING ABOUT IT! Never forget that God isn't moved by tears; HE is only moved by your faith, prayers and action.

Chapter Nine

*Eat Right, Diet,
Exercise*

EAT RIGHT, DIET, EXERCISE

Only saturated fats and dietary cholesterol raise blood cholesterol. A high level of cholesterol in the blood is a major risk factor for coronary heart disease, which leads to heart attack.

— American Heart Association

The single most influential dietary change one can make to lower the risk of these diseases (cardiovascular diseases, diabetes, and certain forms of cancer) is to reduce intake of foods high in fats and to increase the intake of foods high in complex carbohydrates and fiber.

— The Surgeon General Report
on Nutrition & Health, 1982

More than half the adults in the United States of America are over-weight or obese — and the rates of obesity in children and teens have doubled since the late 1970's. Obesity increases the risk of diabetes, heart disease, stroke, and other health problems. Each year in the United States, obesity causes tens of hundreds of thousands of premature deaths, and costs the public over ten billion dollars.

— Center for Disease Control
and Prevention

In 1996 the United States Drug Administration (USDA) replaced its basic four food groups (milk, fruit, meats, vegetables and breads and cereals) with fats, oils and sweets, acknowledging the fact that America had become the land of the doughnut and the home of the french fry. *(see Diagram 1)*

And when the woman saw that the tree was good for food, and that the tree was pleasant to the eye, and a tree to be desired to make one wise, she took of the fruit thereof, and did eat, and gave also unto her husband with her; and he did eat. And the eyes of them were opened, and they knew that they were naked.

— *Gen. 3:6*

Over 53% of people who live in large industrial countries die of heart disease each year.

— *American Medical Journal*

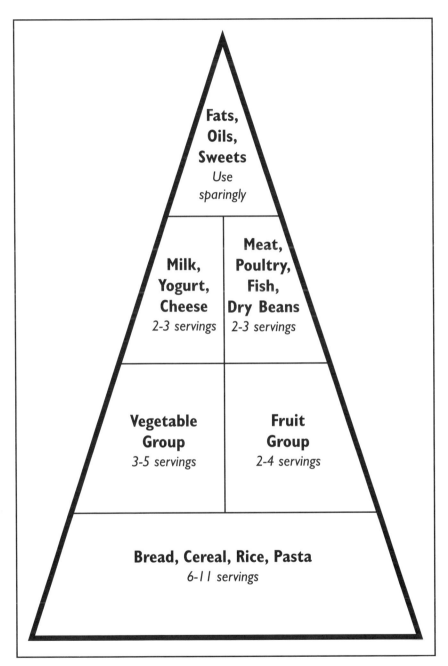

Diagram 1

If you pay close attention you will notice that the food pyramid has two hidden messages in it. The first message to the American public is by decreasing your sweets, fat and oil intake, you will or can increase the intake of the four basic food groups. The second message is that even the *USDA* is aware and acknowledges the obesity levels in our country.

You Really Are What You Eat

*"Good nutrition is the fuel
that drives success."*
— Billy Blanks

Here's something to consider. What good is it to accumulate wealth, make Millions of dollars, become a prosperous and well respected person, if you woke up with a heart attack? How long do you plan to reign on earth with your wealth and prosperity — one year, three years, ten years or twenty years? I don't know about you but I want to enjoy every second, every minute, every hour, every day, every week, every month and every year of my prosperity for the next 100 years. Wait, it's impossible to live that long. **Not if you eat right!**

A Top Achiever's success rate and how fast they achieve their goals is totally depended upon their diets and the foods they eat. If you're not careful and selective about the foods you eat, you can open the door to a number of life-shortening diseases that can take you to an early grave. Typically, most Americans with poor diets suffer from cancer, diabetes, high blood pressure, heart diseases, strokes, bone fractures, and rotting teeth from too much sugar. Recent studies from the State of Michigan Department of Health report shows that Michigan is the number one state in the country for obesity. The study also shows that Detroit is the third largest urban city in America that was considered to be overweight.

Unfortunately, we have become a *microwave-too busy-I'll eat anything-frozen food-fast food-just make sure it's hot* society. The average American has a diet that consists of too much sugar, too much fat, too many calories and even too much protein. We don't know the ingredients of what we are eating. All we know is that it tastes good and we want it super sized. Some of us try to break the cycle by grocery shopping, but we are unaware of the additives, preservatives and the amount of processed foods that are on the shelves. Did you know that more than 50% of the food that you eat is processed in some form or another then placed in a nice shiny wrapper for you to purchase? Some nutritionists estimate that the average product that has been processed has existed at least ten years before it actually hit the shelves of the supermarket.

In America, we are set up to fail when it comes to our diets, health and nutrition. The food industries create the processed foods that we eat, spending an average of **$2 Billion** each year on advertising. Promoting how good something is, how it is good for you, how good it tastes, how hot it is, how spicy it is, how tangy it is, how cheesy it is, how creamy it is, but they never tell how non-nutritional it is for you. Soft drinks, hamburgers, candy, pizza, popcorn, desserts, cheese nachos, and bubble gum are all products that are filled with sugar, fat and enough calories to stop your heart. Did you know that over a 10-year period, you will actually see and hear more than 10,000 hours of advertising to purchase foods that aren't good for you? Then you will see and hear less than 2,000 hours of advertising of products that are actually good for you and have nutritional value that can extend your life span.

Early one Saturday morning, as I lay on the couch watching television, I dozed off for a couple of hours with the television still on. When I woke up, I was starving for something but I didn't know what it was and then it hit me ... *"two all beef patties, special sauce, lettuce, cheese, pickles, onions on a sesame seed bun."* Moments later, I was parked in the drive-thru of McDonald's, waiting on my super-sized Number 2 combo. My plan was to take the combo home but the smell was irresistible. I couldn't wait. I ate the whole thing right there in the car. Around 3:00 p.m. that afternoon, I was hungry again and there was that voice, *"Have it your way, have it have it your way, you can have it your way."* So I went and had it my way, heavy on the pickles and light on the onions. At 10:30 that night, I got a little hungry again. Once more there was that voice again, *"We do chicken right!"* I had my chicken done right at Kentucky Fried Chicken and went on to be a satisfied man.

Has this ever happened to you? Good, then I'm not alone and I don't feel so bad. Do you know what was happening every time I got hungry? My mind connected hunger with commercial jingles. The sweet and seductive advertising temptress would strike, forcing me out of the house against my own will to start my car. She would twist my arm as we drove down the road, then finally sweet-talk me into making a down payment on my death by purchasing a Number 2 combo. That's right, slowly but surely, we are killing our-selves when we decide to eat enormous amounts of foods that aren't nutritionally good for us. It was shocking to me once I realized what was happening. I was working my butt off, day in and day out, to earn money to *kill* myself. Fast food products that are high in sugar and fats kill us in the end and that's the bottom line! A High Achiever with $6 Million in the bank is very insignificant if he's six feet under the ground.

What's the Difference?

*"What I do know can't hurt me
but what I don't know
can kill me."*
— Anon

Half the battle of living stress-free and having a healthy life is understanding what's good for you and what's not good for you. Most of us listen to our friends, coworkers and clips of commercial ads to receive our nutrition information. This form of research can be dangerous because the average person is equally or less informed as you are. Therefore, I felt it was only right to include a simple guide for you to completely understand how and why good nutrition works.

This guide will show you:
- The categories of fat.
- Foods to eat that help heal diseases in your body.
- Healthy tips for healthier eating.
- Myths and commonly asked questions about food.
- How to prepare fun and easy fat-free, low calorie meals.

DIFFERENT FATS

The foods we eat fall in three different categories: Polyunsaturated, Monounsaturated and Saturated Fats. They are typically identified by their fatty acids and chemical structure.

Polyunsaturated Fats are found mainly in nuts, plant seeds and soybeans and they help reduce blood cholesterol levels. The foods that are listed are not necessarily high in fat but they are higher in polyunsaturated fats.

Bagels	Oysters	Sardines
Barbeque sauce	Oatmeal	Scallops
Blue fish	Pine nuts	Sesame seeds
Chickpeas (garbanzo beans)	Popcorn	Soybeans
Cod	Potato chips	Squash
Corn chips	Pumpernickel	Sweet potatoes
Cornmeal	Pumpkin seeds	Tofu
French bread	Rainbow trout	Tuna salad
Haddock	Raisin bread	Vegetables and nut oil
Herring	Refried beans	Walnuts
Italian Bread	Rye bread	Whitefish
Lentils		
Mackerel		
Mussels		

Monounsaturated Fats are found in most foods, but mainly in vegetable oils, such as olive, canola and peanut. These fats are liquid and they reduce total blood cholesterol:

Almonds	Doughnuts	Pecans
Animal fats	Eggs	Pies
Avocados	Fruit cake	Pistachios
Beef	Gingerbread	Popcorn
Bread (most)	Lard	Pork
Brownies	Macadamia nuts	Sausage
Cake	Margarine	Spaghetti
Cashews	Muffins	Tacos
Chestnuts	Oatmeal	Veal
Chicken	Ocean Perch	Vegetable Oil

206

Cookies	Pastries	Vegetable shortening
Croissants	Peanut butter	

Saturated Fats: All meat and dairy products contain saturated fats. Saturated fats are usually solid at room temperature and **they raise total blood cholesterol. These foods are high in saturated fats:**

Beef (fatty cuts)	Cocoa butter	Duck
Beef tallow	Cocoa mixes	Eggnog
Boston brown bread	Coconuts	Fried foods
Butter	Coconut products	(fried in saturated oil)
Cheese	Cottage cheese	Garlic spread
Cheesecake	Cream	Gravy
Chili	Cream soups	Hot dogs (all types)
Chocolate	Custard	Snack cakes
Ice cream	Popcorn	Sour cream
Lamb	Pork	Turkey
Luncheon meats	Pudding	Veal (fatter cuts)
Malts	Quiche	Vegetable and nut oils
Milk	Sauces	
Non dairy creamers	Seaweed	
Non-dairy whipped cream	Shakes	
Pies		
Pizza		
Pompano		

Always remember that the essential fatty acids that we need in our diet are unsaturated, which means that we can get all the fat we need from unsaturated fats. Now here this! There is no biological need for saturated fats. The American Heart Association says that the body can use all three fats but it recommends that daily saturated fat intake be limited to 7 to 10 percent of total calories. Monounsaturated fat intake **should be limited to 15% of total calories. Polyunsaturated fats should be no more than 10 percent of total calories.**

DISEASES
AND
HEALING FOODS

Top Achiever, there is a connection between nutrition and disease. The more nutritionally fit your body becomes, the better your body is able to fight disease. God does not cause anyone to be sick. God is good and good all the time. Think about it! How can God curse you with illness and provide a regenerating mechanism in your body that is so sagacious, it begins to heal every wound, cut, scrape and blemish on your body the moment you injure yourself? The primary reason most Americans have sickness and disease in their body is because of bad nutrition. You don't catch colds, colds are allowed in when there is too much sugar in your system. Did you know that 25 teaspoons of sugar *(25 teaspoons of sugar = 3 to 4 cans of soda)* completely shuts down your immune system within a 24 hour period?

As I travel around the country and speak at different churches, I find that these are the top 10 diseases that the people of God are bound by because of bad nutrition. It's a blessing and amazing to read the testimonies of people who have heard me speak on the topic of nutrition. Most of the individuals who contact me tell me after they have taken my advice and made minor adjustments in their diets that the illnesses in their bodies began to clear up and completely dissipate. **God is so good!** If you have sickness and disease in your body, these foods will help you get rid of it. **Trust me!**

- **ARTHRITIS:** *Fire in the joints and is a condition characterized by joint inflammation, pain, swelling, and redness and causes a limitation in joint movement.*
  Foods: Fatty Fish, Salmon, Herring, Sardines, Albacore Tuna, Extra Virgin Olive Oil, Fresh Fruits, Pineapples, Cherries, Dark Berries, Raisins, Grapes, Fresh Vegetables, Asparagus, Broccoli, Brussels Spouts, Cabbage, Celery, Mustard Greens, Yams, Onions, Nuts, Brazil Nuts, Whole Grains, Ginger, Cinnamon, Oregano, Eggs, Garlic, Legumes, Turmeric.
  Juices: Beet, Cabbage, Carrot, Celery, Cherry, Cucumber, Parsley, Pineapple, and Watermelon.

209

- **ASTHMA:** *Is caused by spasms of the bronchial passages restricting the flow of air in and out of the lungs.*
  Foods: Fresh Fruits, Pineapple, Apricots, Yams, Nuts, Seeds, Whole Grains, Legumes, Fatty Fish, Sardines, Salmon, Albacore Tuna, Mackerel, Chili Peppers, Garlic, Mustard, Onions, Ginger, Turmeric.
  Juices: Carrot, Celery, and Grapefruit.

- **BACK PAIN:** *Acute back pain can result from heavy lifting, misstep, falling, or a sudden motion.*
  Foods: Salmon, Mackerel, Herring, Fresh Fruits, Vegetables, Dark Green Vegetables, Nuts, Whole Grains, Pumpkin Seeds, Walnuts, Ginger, Black Pepper, Extra Virgin Olive Oil, Ground Flax Seeds.
  Juice: Tomato and Grape.

- **BRONCHITIS:** *Is an inflammation of the mucous membrane that lines the breathing or bronchial tubes.*
  Foods: Citrus Fruits, Pineapples, Raspberries, Apricots, Onions, Shiitake Mushrooms, Legumes, Soybeans, Flax Seeds, Salmon, Hot Mustard, Chili Pepper, Horseradish, Albacore Tuna.
  Juices: Beet, Carrot, Cucumber, Radish, Wheatgrass and Spinach.

- **CANCER:** *Cancer develops when changes to the DNA, nucleic acids that are the basis of heredity and contains the genetic blueprint, result in the production of malignant cells that replicate but are not controlled or killed by natural defense mechanisms in the body.*
  Foods: Onions, Ginger, Fish, Herring, Mackerel, Brazil Nuts, Eggs, Fennel, Salmon, Albacore Tuna, Low-Fat Dairy, Low-Fat Yogurt.
  Juices: Apple, Beet, Carrot, Cabbage, Celery, Cherry, Grape, Berry, Spinach and Wheatgrass.

- **DEPRESSION:** *An internal biochemical or hormonal imbalance due to a nutrition deficit.*
  Foods: Whole Organic Foods, Whole Organic Grains, Whole Grain Pasta, Whole Grain Bread, Seafood, Turkey, Nuts, Dried Beans, Melons, Watermelons, Cayenne, Ginger, Dill, Basil.
  Juices: Tomato, Pineapple and Lemon.

- **DIABETES:** *Is a condition where there is too much sugar in the blood and the insulin that is required for processing it is either absent, insufficient, or ineffective.*
  Foods: Whole Grain Breads, Whole Grain Foods, Buckwheat, Brown Rice, Barley, Oats, Lean Meats, Eggs, Fish, Avocados, Rhubarb, Peanuts, Soy Milk, Pears, Broccoli, Lentils, Cabbage, Mushrooms, Spinach, Garlic, Nuts, Bay Leaves, Bitter Melon, Cinnamon.
  Juices: No recommendation.

- **PREMENSTRUAL SYNDROME (PMS):** *Is characterized by symptoms including mood swings, irritability, joint pain, tender breasts, headache and bloating. The cause is likely a hormonal imbalance where too much estrogen is being produced by the body as opposed to the amount of progesterone.*
  Foods: Fresh Foods, Carrots, Dandelion Greens, Whole Grains, Soy Beans, Lima Beans, Black Beans, Peanuts, Nuts, Fish, Seeds, Salmon, Sardines, Mackerel, Extra Virgin Olive Oil, Cold Pressed Organic Canola Oil.
  Juices: Carrot, Cranberry.

- **STRESS:** *Is caused mainly by emotional or psychological situations. The mind affects the body and vice versa.*
  Foods: Fresh Fruit, Honey, Garlic, Salmon, Seafood, Sardines, Pasta, Oats, Yams, Onions, Potatoes, Shiitake Mushrooms, Low Fat Yogurt, Low Fat Dairy.
  Juices: Fruits, Vegetables, Carrot.

- **ULCERS:** *Usually form in the duodenum, the upper part of the small intestine; a peptic ulcer is in the stomach as well as the duodenum. It is so called because of the involvement of pepsin, a digestive enzyme. Ulcers are sores that can bleed. They form when there is too much acid for the mucosal lining to tolerate.*

   Foods: Bananas — stimulate the proliferation of mucosal cells that form a barrier between the lining and acid — Fresh Fruits, Pineapples, Blueberries, Papaya, Fresh Vegetables, Dark Green Leafy Vegetables, Potatoes, Enoki Mushrooms, Whole Grains, Brown Rice, Corn, Legumes (especially Red and White Beans) Seafood, Raw Honey, Garlic, Turmeric, Thyme, Cinnamon, Cardamom, Cloves, Ginger.

   Juices: Cabbage, one-quart daily, strengthens the lining of the stomach and increases mucus activity. Fruit, Vegetable, Carrot, Celery, Kale and Wheatgrass.

HEALTHY TIPS
FOR LIVING
A HEALTHY LIFE

- ☐ Use a reduced-fat or fat-free margarine spread instead of butter. *I Can't Believe It's Not Butter* is my favorite.

- ☐ Use canned evaporated skim milk as a substitute for heavy cream, and low-fat or skim milk in place of whole milk or cream in your recipes.

- ☐ Substitute low-fat, reduced-fat and fat-free cheeses for cheeses that are higher in fat. The fat avoided here is between 6 and 10 grams per ounce!

- ☐ Eat whole wheat bread with most of your meals. It's better for you.

- ☐ Cut out all excess sugar in your diet.

- ☐ Stop eating ribs, pork sausage, pork chops, bacon and gizzards; **basically all pork products.**

- ☐ When putting together a macaroni, potato, tuna, or turkey salad, don't forget to use fat-free or reduced-fat mayonnaise.

- ☐ For desserts, splurge on occasion, but substitute something. Buy sugarless cookies, sugarless cakes, sugarless brownies and use low-fat Cool Whip and fruit.

- ☐ Take raw almonds and raw nuts and pour raw honey over it for the great taste of a candy bar.

- ☐ Don't eat peanut butter and jelly sandwiches on white bread. Use wheat bread and use cashew butter instead or almond butter and sugarless jelly (strawberry) on whole wheat bread.

☐ Familiarize yourself with the number of fat grams and the percentage of calories from fat in the foods you eat most often, so that it becomes second nature to compute your fat consumption.

☐ For breakfast, eat whole wheat grain cereals with soy milk (vanilla).

☐ Avoid hot dogs of any kind (even turkey); they have too much fat.

☐ Don't eat corned beef; it's too fatty.

☐ Cut out all organ meats in your diet.

☐ Use a light brand of sour cream or plain non-fat yogurt on top of your food.

☐ Use ground turkey instead of ground hamburger.

☐ When having fried chicken remove all the skin, shake it up in whole wheat flour and fry it in olive oil.

☐ Reduce the amount of melted butter in your diet by a third or a half.

☐ Instead of whole eggs, use egg whites to make omelets and scrambled eggs.

☐ Use partly-skimmed ricotta instead of full-fat cream cheese for luscious cheesecake.

☐ Instead of pan-frying or deep-frying, bake or broil meat, fish, poultry and baste it in wine, lemon, or tomato juice, broth, or low-fat or fat-free salad dressing to keep it from drying out.

☐ When using oil, make sure it's the least saturated type available.

☐ Instead of preparing a pan with cooking oil or shortening, use a nonstick pan sprayed with a small amount of cooking spray. Or spread a small amount of oil over the surface of the pan with a paper towel.

☐ Try to have dinner before 7:00 p.m. because your metabolism is running at a much slower rate at the end of the day.

☐ Make sure you have breakfast to get your metabolism started.

☐ Use powdered low-fat or skim milk instead of non-dairy creamer.

☐ Budget your fat grams.

☐ Have at least one piece of raw fruit per day (apple, oranges, grapes).

☐ Gradually reduce the salt that you use in your cooking.

☐ Prepare salads just before they are going to be served.

☐ Eat a green leafy vegetable every day.

☐ Broil or boil potatoes instead of frying potatoes in oil.

☐ Eliminate soft drinks from your diet.

- [ ] Start reading the labels on all processed foods that you buy.

- [ ] Try different combinations of food to create different sweet flavors without adding sugar.

- [ ] Steer completely clear of french fries.

Now I know you may be saying, "Jonathan's book is pretty good, but this guy is crazy. I can't do this!" YES YOU CAN!

MYTHS
AND
COMMONLY ASKED
QUESTIONS

<u>Commonly Asked Questions</u>

☐ **Do calories from one type of food make you fatter than those from another?** No, all calories count. Sorry.

☐ **Why is sugar bad for me?** Sugar decays your teeth and breaks down your immune system.

☐ **Can eating carbohydrates help me lose weight?** Yes, if eaten properly.

☐ **Are carbohydrates good for diabetics?** Yes, if you have a diet high in *complex* carbohydrates.

☐ **Is whole wheat bread better than white bread?** Yes, whole wheat bread provides your body with the fiber it needs.

☐ **Can I have too much protein?** Yes, if you eat more protein than the body needs, the excess nitrogen is excreted and stored for fat.

☐ **How much protein should I feed my children?** A child needs three times the amount of protein than adults.

☐ **Should I have protein everyday?** Yes, the body cannot store protein. It needs a new supply daily.

☐ **If I have too much protein, what effects should I expect?** You can expect liver and kidney damage, easily broken bones or fractures.

☐ **Should I take vitamins?** Yes, vitamins provide nutritional supplements for your body.

☐ **What are food additives?** Synthetic copies of processed foods.

☐ **Should I change my diet as I get older?** Yes, you should lower the amount of food you take in each year.

☐ **Is coffee bad for me?** Yes, it causes the secretion of acids in the body.

☐ **Are eggs bad for me?** Yes, if not eaten properly, they are very high in cholesterol.

☐ **What are high cholesterol meats?** Bacon, ham hocks, pig's feet, pig ears, pork butt, picnic shoulder ham, and spareribs.

☐ **Is using half and half in my coffee all right?** No, half and half contains 12% butterfat.

☐ **What can I use instead of sour cream?** Non-fat yogurt. The taste isn't too much different and it is healthier for you.

☐ **Is chewing gum bad for me?** Yes, gum contains large amounts of sugar and it sends false signals to the body.

☐ **How do I know if the food contains what I need?** Read the label. It's the law that manufacturing food companies must list the nutritional information on the back of the package.

☐ **Is alcohol good for me?** Yes, but not all alcohols. Red or dark wine is the best because it gets into the blood stream and causes your blood to flow, which is good for the heart.

☐ **Is bottled water better than tap water?** No, only unprocessed water from a natural spring or brook is free of any impurities. Tip: If a bottle of water says spring fresh, spring pure, spring type, it's not spring water at all but rather it's processed tap or well water. Sorry.

☐ **How many calories do I need?** A woman weighing 120 pounds needs about 2,000 calories. A man weighing 150 pounds needs between 2,000 to 2,400 calories for daily activity.

☐ **Which is better ice water or water at room temperature?** Water at room temperature because ice water is more difficult for the body to digest.

☐ **What is the fastest way for me to lose weight?** I don't know. Everyone's metabolism and bodies are different.

☐ **If I become a vegetarian will I lose weight?** Yes, but there are some overweight vegetarians.

☐ **What in the world is fructose?** Fructose is fruit sugar, the sweetest of commonly used sweeteners, and the monosaccharide that naturally predominates in most fruits. Although it can satisfy your sweet tooth, it can cause diarrhea and abdominal pain.

FAT FREE
RECIPES

Good Eating with Jonathan

Jonathan's Low-Cholesterol French Toast

Ingredients:

2 eggs and 2 egg whites
1/4 cup skim milk
1/2 teaspoon cinnamon
1/4 teaspoon salt

8 slices of whole wheat bread
Freshly cut strawberries
Low calorie or sugarless syrup

Take a large mixing bowl and mix the eggs, egg whites, milk, cinnamon, and salt with a wired whisk. Take the slices of whole wheat bread and dip into the mixture. Take a pan that has been sprayed with PAM or a hot griddle that has been lightly greased with vegetable oil and place the wheat toast in it allowing to brown on both sides. Take the freshly cut strawberries and garnish. (Fruit choice is optional. Strawberries are my favorite.) If you must use butter, use *I Can't Believe It's Not Butter*. Yields 2 servings. Enjoy!

Jonathan's High-Protein Grilled Chicken Breast Omelets

Ingredients:

2 skinless boneless chicken breast
4 egg whites
1/4 cup skim milk
1/4 teaspoon salt
1/4 teaspoon black pepper
1 diced Roma tomato
1/4 teaspoon thyme

1 freshly cut green pepper
1 freshly cut red pepper
1/2 cup Shiitake mushrooms
1 finely diced yellow onion
1/4 cup low-fat Colby cheese
1/2 cup low-fat Italian dressing
Half of a fresh lemon

Take a mixing bowl and mix the egg whites, salt, pepper, and milk together with a wired whisk or fork. Then in a separate bowl, immerse your chicken breast into the low-fat Italian dressing and sprinkle with thyme. Squeeze the lemon juice in the bowl and allow the chicken to marinate for a minimum of 10 minutes. Heat a pan or skillet that has been greased with vegetable oil. Place the chicken breast in the skillet and pour the marinade in as well. Then place a meat press or a bowl on top of the chicken. Brown the chicken on both sides and cook thoroughly. Then cut the chicken breast into fine strips and place to the side. In a separate skillet that has been sprayed with PAM pour the egg white mixture. Once the egg whites have cooked (not for too long), place the strips of chicken breast in the middle along with the onions, green peppers, red peppers, mushrooms, tomatoes and cheese. Fold the omelet over and allow it to cook to your satisfaction. Remove and serve with freshly cut fruit and cranberry juice. Yields 2 servings. Delicious!

Email me and tell me what you think!

Jonathan's Sweet Summer Fruit Plate

Ingredients:

1 small watermelon
1 papaya
1 honey dew
2 Granny Smith apples
1 large cantaloupe
2 cups low-fat yogurt

1 pineapple
2 crates fresh strawberries
4 bananas
2 fresh kiwi
1/4 cup sun-dried raisins
4 peaches

With a sharp knife cut up all of the fruit and place it on a large serving tray. Take the low-fat yogurt and place it in a bowl in the center of the tray. Take the sun-dried raisins, sprinkle over the top of the yogurt and dig in. This fruit tray is perfect for entertaining guests in the summertime. It's simple and delicious.

Jonathan's Hot & Tasty Turkey Sub

Ingredients:

1 package ground turkey meat
1 package whole wheat submarine
  buns
1 tomato
1/4 teaspoon salt
1/4 cup low-fat Italian dressing
1 tablespoon olive oil

1 head lettuce
1 yellow onion
1/4 teaspoon cayenne pepper
1 bell pepper, thinly sliced
1/4 teaspoon black pepper
1/2 cup water

Place the entire package of ground turkey in a pre-heated pan that has been greased with olive oil or PAM cooking spray. In a bowl, mix the Italian dressing, black pepper, cayenne pepper, bell pepper, salt, and onions together. After the ground turkey has cooked thoroughly, add other ingredients and stir. Pour in 1/2 cup of water and let simmer for 5 minutes. Place the whole wheat buns in the oven and allow to warm. Then take the turkey mix, place it inside the bun, and garnish with lettuce and tomato (low-fat cheese optional). Yields 4 servings. It's smoking!

Jonathan's Humming Hummus
(Chickpea Spread)

Ingredients:

1 large onion
1 to 2 cloves garlic, minced
2 tablespoons vegetable oil
2 cups chickpeas (garbanzos)
  (if canned, drain and rinse)
1/2 cup fresh lemon juice

1 tablespoon soy sauce
1/2 teaspoon salt
1/4 cup sesame paste
1/2 cup sesame seeds, toasted
  and ground

Sauté the onion and garlic in the oil until they are soft and set aside. In a food processor or blender, puree the chickpeas with the onion and garlic and the remaining ingredients. Yields 3 cups. This is excellent with whole wheat pita bread cut up into diamonds (warm bread if possible).

Jonathan's Succulent Salmon & Potatoes

Ingredients:

2 fresh pieces of salmon
1 lemon
2 teaspoon olive oil
1/4 teaspoon thyme
1 tablespoon low-fat yogurt

8 large red potatoes
1/4 teaspoon salt
1/4 cup scallions
1/4 teaspoon garlic salt

Preheat oven to 350°. Place salmon on baking sheet and sprinkle salt, garlic salt, thyme, lemon juice and olive oil over the top. Cover with aluminum foil and bake 20 minutes. Cut up potatoes with skin and boil 20 minutes. Garnish potatoes with scallions and low-fat yogurt. Eat your heart out!

I hope these recipes are a blessing to your life!
Jonathan Edison

Go to **www.jonathanedisonspeaks.com** and shop online.

The Importance of Exercise

"The body is the extension of the mind."
— Lee Haney

As we strive to live a life of abundance and become individuals who are looked upon as geniuses because of our hard work, diligence and commitment, we must develop the mindset of **our physical being our mental**. Mental competence will take you far, but staying physically fit will keep you going. Eighty-five percent of what we do in life is mental and the other fifteen percent is physical. You can't have 85% of your mental working for you and only .5% of your physical in action. We cannot afford to neglect our physical activity regiments because they provide us with the strength and endurance we need to help us reach our goals. Physical health is more important than wealth, fame and success. "But I'm on a diet!" Fantastic, but you still need to have some type of physical activity in your life. Walking, jogging, running stairs, weight training, cycling, bowling, golfing, swimming or anything that requires you to put forth an effort.

Now you don't have to become a workout junkie or fanatic. You just have to get some exercise into your life. Why? It reduces tension, stress and anxiety that you may suffer from in attempting to achieve maximum success for your life. I exercise a minimum of three days out of the week and I feel great afterwards. I look at the weights and envision the person who got on my nerves that day and I start pushing them around. When I get on the treadmill and run, I spend time focusing and visualizing my dream coming to pass in my mind's eye. As I use dumbbells to do my curls, I pretend that they are large bags of gold that have been left for me. When I punch the punching bag, I imagine myself knocking out my enemy who has done me wrong. As I do my leg lifts, I think about how much butt I'm going to need to kick to reach my goals. Finally, as I start my sit-ups, I think about that person who was trying to hold me back from my Millions and I laugh each time my back comes up off the floor.

Exercising is not only good for you physically, it's good for you spiritually as well. Every three or four days, I take time to jog near a body of water early in the morning. I can't explain the peace and tranquility that fills my spirit. I often close my eyes and pretend that God is right there with me. I know God is omnipresent, but when I close my eyes and start communicating with Him, it's one of the most beautiful feelings in the world to have Him running alongside me, whispering in my ear.

Top Achiever, I can't stress enough how important physical activity is to your peace of mind. As a former personal trainer and spa owner, I was fortunate enough to have a high-end clientele of lawyers, doctors, corporate executives and rich housewives who all were under a tremendous amount of stress. After their workouts, they said pretty much the same thing, "Jonathan, I don't know how I would make it through the week without your workouts. It's fun, it relieves my stress and it makes me feel good." Therefore, as you strive to make Millions and stay stress free, allow me to share a few of the workouts with you. Here's the great thing about the workout: you can do them right at home in your living room or, if you're on the road traveling, you can perform them in the hotel.

* Anytime you take on a new physical activity program, you should consult with a physician first.
* To reduce the risk of injury, be sure to stretch before and after each workout.

Jonathan's Millionaire
30-Minute Workouts for a Stress-Free Life!

Day 1
(30-minute workout)

Cardiovascular Routine

2 sets of 20 jumping jacks
2 sets of 20 squats
2 sets of 20 kick-backs
2 sets of 20 leg swings
  (standing straight up and
  kicking your leg toward the
  ceiling, one at a time)
Note: While performing this
exercise you should hold on
to a chair or prop.

2 sets of 10 pushups
4 sets of 10 sit-ups
4 sets of 10 crunches

  March in place for
  5 minutes to cool down.

Day 2
(30-minute workout)

Upper Body Routine

4 sets of 10 push ups
4 sets of 10 front laterals
2 sets of 10 arm curls
2 sets of 25 right hand air punches
2 sets of 20 crunches

4 sets of 10 side laterals
  (with phone books)
4 sets of 10 triceps extensions
2 sets of 25 left hand
  air punches

March in place for 5 minutes cool down

Day 3
(30-minute workout)

Lower Body Routine

4 sets of 10 squats
4 sets of 20 calf raises
4 sets of 10 step-ups
 (on a chair or bed)
2 sets of 15 sit-ups
Jog in place for 3 minutes
 then walk in place for 2 minutes

2 sets of 10 lunges
2 sets of 25 bicycle kicks
 (while lying on your back)
2 sets of 10 leg lifts
 (lying on your back with
 both feet together).

Day 4
REST!!

Day 5
SAME AS DAY 1

But I Can't Find The Time

"What good is it being a
Millionaire in memory?"
— Kristal Cooper

Don't tell me you're too busy to exercise because we find the time to do everything else that we want to do. Like six hours of shopping, 20 hours of watching television, 40 hours of sleeping, five hours of gossiping, 12 hours of driving and 15 hours of eating, and that's just in one week. What do you mean you can't find the time to workout? You better find the time to diet and exercise because if you don't, you're preparing yourself for an early grave. As soon as you think it's important, it will be too late. The grim reaper will be at your door paying you a visit.

Are you familiar with a great man of our time by the name of Reginald F. Lewis?

Reginald Lewis was born in 1942 and grew up in a middle class neighborhood in Baltimore, Maryland. Lewis won a football scholarship to Virginia State College (now Virginia State University) and graduated with a degree in economics in 1965. He attended Harvard Law School and graduated in 1968. After working at several law firms, Lewis opened TLC Group, a venture capital firm. In 1987, Lewis bought Beatrice International Foods for $985 Million and created TLC Beatrice, a snack food, beverage, and grocery store conglomerate that was the largest black-managed business in the United States. At its peak in 1996, TLC Beatrice had sales of $2.2 Billion and was number 512 on *Fortune Magazine's* list of 1,000 largest companies. Lewis was a prominent philanthropist. His financial gift of $3 Million to Harvard Law School was the largest single donation the school had received and created the Reginald F. Lewis Fund for International Study and Research. In 1991, he was considered to be the richest black man in the country. Unfortunately, at the tender age of 51, Reginald Lewis passed away due to a life of stress and lack of exercise.

CHAPTER TEN

Work Your Money!
Don't Let It Work You

Do You Know Money?

*"Money doesn't talk,
it screams!"*
— Clara Luper

The first key and law of learning anything is to know the basics and the history of it. In our case, we are seeking riches and wealth, so let me explain the basics and a little history on the subject of money.

Money is a piece of paper that measures 2 5/8 by 6 1/8 inches, with a thickness of .0043 inches. The U.S. Department of the Treasury first issued paper U.S. currency in 1862 to make up for the shortage of coins and to finance the Civil War. There was a shortage of coins because people had started hoarding them. The uncertainty caused by the war had made the value of items fluctuate drastically. Because coins were made of gold and silver, their value didn't change much. Nevertheless, people wanted to hang onto them rather than buy items that might lose their value. The first paper notes were printed in denominations of 1 cent, 5 cents, 25 cents, and 50 cents. Today, money is currently created in two different forms, coins and currency. Coins are usually made of copper and a second element, such as zinc or nickel. Currency paper is composed of 25 percent linen and 75 percent cotton. Red and blue synthetic fibers of various lengths are distributed evenly throughout the paper. Before World War I, these fiber were made of silk.

The U.S. Government is responsible for creating and monitoring the supply of available currency in this country. At one time, banks were permitted to issue their own paper bills as long as they kept a portion of the bank's savings with the government. However, banks soon began to issue currency with so many different face values that the situation became unwieldy. At one point, there were over a thousand different types of paper money in circulation.

In addition to manufacturing money, the federal government is responsible for monitoring how much money is in circulation. Approximately $333 BILLION is in circulation today. Thirty-eight Million notes a day with the face value of approximately $541 Million are printed every day. As money wears out or is damaged, it is returned to the Treasury through a network of intermediaries. The Federal Reserve Banks shreds damaged or worn out money daily to the tune of MILLIONS and MILLIONS of dollars each year.

Did you know ... If you used $1 bills, a MILLION DOLLARS would weigh 2,040.8 pounds, but if you used $100 bills it would weigh 20.4 pounds?

Did you know ... If you had 10 Billion $1 notes and spent one note every second of every day, it would require 317 years for you to go broke?

Can I Be Rich and Still Be A Christian?

"Money helps, it doesn't hurt"
— Anon

One of the most common misconceptions that many Americans have who confess to love God is that money is evil and only the evil people become rich. This type of thinking has been passed down from generation to generation and is the one biggest tricks of the enemy to keep you sick, broke and in poverty. Are you familiar with the word charity? This word is a word that a lot of Christians forget about when the subject of being rich and wealthy comes up.

A good man or woman of God is supposed to be able to take a friend or someone in trouble and put them up in a hotel for seven days and pay with CASH; provide the meals for that person for seven days and pay with CASH; provide that person with transportation money or a rental car and pay with CASH. Then pay all of the incidentals on the room in CASH. On the seventh day, if it is necessary, go back and do it all over again for another seven days. How many people do you know that can afford that ticket?

How many people do you know that say they love God? This is why it's so important to break the cycle of thinking that being broke brings you closer to God. Being rich brings you closer to God I told you in the beginning that God is good and it is good to be rich. The ability to help someone else in need is more powerful than planning and setting up a Pity Party for them. Understand and know that God wants you to be rich so that you will be able to serve Him better. It takes money to do everything that you do in life and you can't do anything in life broke. Stop listening to the foolish idea and tradition that says people who say they love God shouldn't have any money. Get all of the money you can and bless somebody else's house. Then sit back and watch how the Kingdom of God works through you.

Can You Pass The Test?

*"Money is just like school,
it's Elementary but the test is
always multiple choice."*
— Dr. Leroy Thompson

In order for you to have complete dominance over money and it not have dominance over you, you're going to have to pass the Money Test. What's the Money Test? I'm glad you asked. The Money Test deals with your wants, desires, needs and self control. Can you go inside of a mall and not spend any money? Are you the type of person that needs to purchase something everyday? Are you a compulsive shopper? Does money come into your hands and fly right out of the window? Have you ever looked in your wallet or purse and said, "Man!! I didn't realize I'd spent so much?" Yes? So have I. A few years ago, I was in the same boat with Millions of other Americans who couldn't pass the Money Test. How do I pass the Money Test? The only way to pass the Money Test is to **STOP SHOPPING!** Don't close the book yet. Allow me to explain.

Maybe you should go and get a glass of water right now. Just kidding! Have you ever heard of the phrase, **"It takes money to make money"**? Well, it's true. It takes the money that you refuse to spend at the mall, the club, the bar and anywhere else that you spend unnecessarily. You could probably save over $500 a month or more in some cases, if you stop spending money on unnecessary items. Ask yourself before you purchase something. Do you really need it or are you just buying it to satisfy a need and desire to shop? Seven out of ten times, the answer will be no, you don't need it. The good thing is that when an opportunity presents itself for you to make Millions of dollars, you will have the capital to help it get started. I told you there was no magic wand. It's up to you to make the choice to plan for your future by saving and passing Money Tests.

What's the Secret to Money?

*"The only thing you can learn by
studying poverty is how to be poor."*
— Michael Novak

The secret to money is that there is no secret. Most wealthy individuals will tell you that there are principles and procedures to wealth that must to be followed and carried out with diligence and preciseness. The first procedure that I would suggest is to get a copy of all of your credit reports.

Listed below are the "big three" credit bureaus:

Equifax
Credit Information Services
P.O. Box 105496
Atlanta, GA 30348-5496
800/997-2493
www.equifax.com

Experian
National Consumer Assistance
P.O. Box 2104
Allen, TX 75013
888/Experian
www.experian.com

Trans Union LLC
Consumer Disclosure Center
P.O. Box 1000
Chester, PA 19022
800/888-4213
www.transunion.com

This is extremely important because sometimes "humans" make mistakes and once you read over your statements, you may find a few human errors. If so, the next step is to get it taken care of as soon as possible. When I graduated from college, I was under the assumption that my credit was pretty decent. I paid my bills on time the majority of the time, and I didn't have any outstanding debt such as a car or home. To my surprise, when I tried to purchase my first vehicle, I was turned down because of a low credit score.

Most of us are used to the term "BAD CREDIT," but the proper term is a low credit score. This is another trick of the enemy to keep you off balance and in debt. No one likes to read anything bad about themselves. Subconsciously, we deny the fact that we should review our credit report and we just go through life assuming that everything is fine. What I found out after I reviewed my credit report was surprising. A gentleman with the same last name and first initial as mine had showed up on my credit report, therefore, bringing my credit score down.

It took a couple of months and a lot of phone calls, but I finally got my credit report straightened out. The individuals who work at the credit bureaus are there to help and serve you. Put them to work and order a copy of your credit report today. Once you receive your report, go over it and check for all discrepancies. If you find any information that isn't correct, contact the credit bureau and the creditor and have it corrected immediately.

Are There Enough Millions For Me Too?

*"It is the first duty of every
man not to be poor."*
— Sophie Tucker

Sometimes it's hard to even imagine that you can acquire Millions of dollars because of the mental conditioning we have received throughout our lives. We have been told from our friends, parents, relatives, teachers and even some preachers that it's impossible to make a Million Dollars. The common myth is that the only way for an individual to make a Million Dollars is to play professional sports or to have Bill Gates as a stepfather. However, since we all can't play professional sports or be related to Bill Gates, we must use our own creative skills and talents.

The Selig Center for Economic Growth reported that in 1996-1997 the nation's total buying power rose from **$4 TRILLION** to almost **$6 TRILLION**. In the African American community alone, we have a buying power of about **$800 BILLION**. In the Hispanic community, there is close to **$300 BILLION** of buying power. Do the math and you will figure out that there is a lot of money being spent in the United States of America every year.

Now all that you have to do is figure out a way to tap into it. Remember those dreams and goals we talked about in the earlier chapters? Now you can put them to work.

Yeah, but how can I become a MILLIONAIRE? I'm glad you asked. If you invent, create, or come up with anything that can be sold to children, you can be a MILLIONAIRE practically instantly. **BUT HOW?** I'm glad you asked. In the State of California alone, there are approximately 900,000 children from ages 3-18. Let's just say you wrote a 15-page children's book and sold it to the California school district for $3 a copy.

Do the math!

Let's say you don't like to write and your talent and gift is cooking. **Fantastic!** Create a healthy treat that children love and sell it to the California School District. Not to mention the other thousands of school districts across the country. Let's say you can't cook and you don't like to write. That's fine too! Create something as simple as a yo-yo that kids love and you can become a MILLIONAIRE! Remember we're talking about the entire country buying your product. **START THINKING BIG!!!**

You know, sometimes part of the problem is that we think our ideas are silly, stupid or too simple to make us rich. **NOT TRUE!** There is a woman right now who lives in Texas that will beg to differ. This woman was pregnant and her husband wasn't home, so she decided to order a take out salad from one of her favorite restaurants. When she opened up the box and tried to eat the salad, she found it really difficult because the lettuce and tomatoes were in large pieces. She had to run to the kitchen and use a sharp steak knife and fork to cut up her salad. Several days later, she ordered another salad from a different restaurant and the same thing occurred. She became so frustrated that she called her husband at work and told him what happened. Then she decided to do something about it. "Honey, wouldn't it be great to have something to cut up your salad with instead of a knife and fork?"

I know this sounds silly, but wait until you read what happened. Her husband agreed and they used $2,000 of their savings and designed a salad chopper. It looks like a pair of ice tongs, but it has blades on the end that cut the salad when you squeeze it repeatedly. Several months later on the

Internet, she had sold over 600,000 of her salad choppers at $14.99 a unit. **Do the Math!** Her company is so lucrative that her husband quit his job and he now works for her. **Not too shabby for a pregnant housewife with an appetite.**

In GOD We Trust

"Children, how hard is it
for them that trust in riches
to enter into the kingdom of God!"
— Mark 10:24

Keep in mind not to trust in money, but to trust in God. Sometimes we get so caught up in trying to make money that we forget about who actually created it. God is the creator of all things and He has the master key to the entire Universe. Trust in Him that He will lead you down the right path. Trust in Him that He would give you the witty invention during prayer. Trust in Him that He will protect you as you travel around the country. Trust in Him that He controls the economy and the flow of currency in the entire world. Trust in Him that money is an elementary thing and He is the teacher. Trust in Him that He can make you rich and prosperous. Trust in Him because He is the God of more than enough and He's already rich.

Happiness to every natural father in the world is to see their children living an abundant life of health and wealth. God wants to see the same for all of His sons and daughters as well. The fastest way to access wealth is through prayer first. When you spend time with God on a regular and consistent basis He will give you the answer that you have been seeking. Nothing is too hard for Him and money is the easiest.

Speak Wealth Into Your Life

*"Put your dream on your
tongue and spit it out like fire."*
— T.D. Jakes

For many years, because of our different cultures and the teaching we received from our parents and grandparents, we are quiet, timid and meek about our dreams, goals and aspirations. My grandmother used to say to me, "Boy, don't tell anybody what you're doing because you might jinx yourself," or "Boy, keep that information close to your chest. You don't want anything bad to happen to you before you do it." This type of mindset and mental conditioning had me in bondage for years. The same way it has Millions of Americans today. We've been tricked to be quiet, to shut up and not to say anything because, deep down inside, we fear success.

Psychologists say that the average human being has between 30 and 50,000 thoughts per day and a minimum of four ideas a year that can create financial wealth beyond belief. With those odds, how in the world can you make the excuse not to say anything because you thought somebody was going to steal your idea? Try to understand that by speaking your thoughts, ideas and dreams into the Universe, you are giving God permission to help, aid and assist you. **But what if my idea and dream is crazy? SO!**

In my local paper one morning, the headline read, "Young Man Running for MAYOR: Does he have a chance?" I thought to myself, "Wow! Who is this guy?" His name was Kwame Kilpatrick, a 31-year-old young man with a dream of becoming mayor in the great city of Detroit. A few weeks later, I read an article which read, "Young man running for mayor. It's obvious that he doesn't have a chance because he's putting out his campaign materials too early. He has overbudgeted and he's short staffed. We hope he learns from his mistakes in the future." That same young man is the honorable mayor of the city of Detroit.

After his inauguration, I read an article in the news that quoted the new mayor saying, "To most it seemed a little crazy, even ridiculous for a young man my age to even entertain the thought of running for mayor. We had an untraditional campaign and the funny thing is that the same people who called me crazy NOW CONSIDER ME A GENIUS."

How did this happen for him? That's amazing! No, it's simple. **He prayed and said with his mouth** what he wanted to do and he did it with the help of God, close friends and family. **Congratulations, Mr. Mayor!** You are a soldier and an example to the world. "Right Here, Right Now." Always remember that God has ALL power and if you ask Him to come into your life and give you the strength, He will.

"MY HEART is inditing a
good matter: I speak of the
things which I have made touching
the king: my tongue is the pen
of a ready writer."
— Ps. 45:1

Do You Have A Budget?

*"A fool and his money
will soon depart."*
— Scripture

For some of us, the most integral parts of our lives have become money and our inconsistency to control it. We go through life haphazardly and we never take the time to do something as simple as a weekly or monthly budget. Creating a personal budget serves several purposes. It allows you to manage the money you have now and prepare for the Millions that you will have in the future. It is impossible for you to accumulate wealth and keep it if you don't know how to budget your spending.

The first step is to sit down in a nice quiet place and take a look at all of your bills. Second, write down how much money you're bringing into your home and how much money is going out. Finally, you should create a record keeping system that shows you where you stand financially. A good budget will show both weekly and monthly expenses. This allows you to really stay on top of your spending and your earning. In creating your budget, keep in mind that it's important to stick to it for your own good. Without a budget you run the risk of overspending and spending unnecessary money.

Are You Living A Credit Card Fantasy?

*"If you don't have it, you
shouldn't spend it."*
— Anon

It's the new money of the 21st Century that allows us to rent cars, rent hotel rooms, make reservations, go on vacations, shop online, shop in department stores, buy gas and buy food with just a swipe. What is it? The **CREDIT CARD**. I admit they are convenient at times but they are also dangerous if not used properly. Most Millionaires only use credit cards when it's necessary or it provides them convenience. For example, purchasing tickets to sporting events, hotel reservations and online shopping. Primarily, most Millionaires operate on a cash basis. It is estimated that Americans charge over $600 Billion on their credit cards each year. Be extremely careful with your credit cards because you don't want to extend yourself by spending beyond the funds that you have. Credit card interest rates will drain your finances without you even realizing it.

How do I get control of my credit card debt? It's simple: **STOP SPENDING** and pass the test. If you must purchase an item, try to use cash as often as possible. Also pay your credit card bills on time because late payment fees are not cheap and if you continue to pay late, it will lower your credit rating.

How To Increase Your Wealth

"Give and it shall be given unto;
good measure, pressed down, and
shaken together, and running over
shall men give into your bosom."
— Luke 6:38

The entire planet is based on this spiritual law. What you give to life is what you get from life. God is a giving God and He expects you to give also. Therefore, you must give ten percent of your earnings to God by tithing. It is the first fruit of your wages. If you expect to increase your wealth, the first principle is to sow seeds that benefit others. Be a blessing to a family, church, school, organization, a group of children or just someone who is in need of assistance. When you give to someone else, you release your Angel to go and bring you more wealth. There is a prerequisite you have to pass before you can benefit from this Godly system of exchange. If you give, it cannot be out of necessity. The giving that you do should come from your heart. If it's not from your heart, you will bless someone else and cancel out your own blessing.

How do I know if it's from my heart? How do I know whom to bless? What should I bless them with? The answer is in prayer. God will touch your heart and give you specific instructions on who to bless and what to bless them with. Don't underestimate the power of prayer.

Always Remain Humble

"Yea, all of you be subject
one to another, and be
clothed with humility."
— I Pet. 5:5

I've interviewed a various number of Millionaires for the research of this book and 90% of them shared with me the advice to always remaining humble. They felt that achieving your goals with confidence and knowing who you are is important. But in the framework of achieving wealth and prosperity, it is essential to understand that everything you accumulate can be taken from you in a matter of seconds. A man who cannot humble himself is a dangerous man to himself. Most people look at humility as a form of weakness but in actuality it depicts one of the greatest forms of strength. Have you seen a man or woman of great wealth and affluence give a speech or talk and before the speech begins, the person is so overwhelmed that they actually shed a tear or two? How did you feel about that? Did you instantly feel a strong connection with that speaker? Notice what happened once that speaker released his or her humility. They instantly gained more power of love, respect and favor from God and the audience.

No one likes a cocky, arrogant, disrespectful, prideful person and it doesn't matter if you have $10,000 or $10 Million. If you're not humble within yourself and to other people, you stand the risk of losing it all. What's one way to be humble? I learned this from my mentor who has hundreds of Millions of Dollars. Every time we are out somewhere and someone stops us to compliment his beautiful $450,000 gold-toned convertible Rolls Royce Corniche, he doesn't grumble or turn his nose up at him or her. He simply acknowledges them and says, "Thank you, my friend. God is so good and I appreciate that comment. I wish I had a little more time because I would let you take it for a spin." It's amazing that something so simple can make the world a better place where individuals can live in prosperity and not be full of themselves. Staying humble and walking in God's power is the safest thing for you to do. Here's a story that one of my Millionaire buddies emailed me that I refer to from time to time concerning humility.

The Brick

A young successful executive was traveling down a neighborhood street, going a bit too fast in his new Jaguar. He was watching out for children, in case one darted out from between parked cars, and slowed down when he thought he saw something. As his car passed, no children appeared. Instead, he heard something smash into his Jag's side door! He slammed on the brakes, put the car in reverse and returned to the spot where the brick was thrown. The angry driver then jumped out of the car, grabbed the nearest little boy and pushed him up against a parked car shouting, "What was all that about and who are you? Just tell me what the heck are you doing? That's a new car and that brick you threw is going to cost a lot of money. Why did you do it?"

The young boy was apologetic. "Please, Mister ... please. I'm sorry, but I didn't know what else to do," he pleaded. "I threw the brick because no one else would stop ..." With tears dripping down his chin, the young boy pointed to a spot just around a parked car. "It's my brother," he said. "He rolled off the curb and fell out of his wheelchair and I'm too weak to lift him up." Now sobbing, the boy asked the stunned executive, "Would you please help me get him back into his wheelchair? He's hurt and he's too heavy for me."

Moved beyond words, the driver tried to swallow the rapid swelling in his throat. He hurriedly lifted the handi-

capped boy back into the wheelchair, then took out his hand-
kerchief and dabbed at the fresh scrapes and cuts. A quick
look told him everything was going to be okay. "Thank you
and may God bless you," the grateful child told the executive. Too shook up for words, the man simply watched the
boy push his wheelchair-bound brother down the sidewalk
toward their home.

It was a long, slow walk back to the Jaguar. The damage
was noticeable, but the driver never went to repair the dent-
ed side door. He kept the dent there to remind himself "not
to go through life so fast and full of yourself that someone
has to throw a brick to get your attention!" God whispers in
our souls and speaks to our hearts so that we may remain
humble, prosperous and stress-free.

<u>Tips for Getting Out of Debt</u>

- Avoid using your credit card on small items.
- Pay off your lowest debt first, then work on the other ones.
- Never spend more than you earn.
- Try to live off 10% of your total income.
- Make sure you pay all of your bills on time.
- The first time you fall behind on your payment, revisit your budget and make the necessary adjustments.
- Develop a plan to put away money for a rainy day.
- Order a copy of your credit report and go over it thoroughly.
- Buy bargain brands of food when you shop.
- You may even have to trade your car in for a smaller one.
- Don't borrow any more money until you pay off your debts.
- You may have to move to a smaller living space to reduce your living costs.
- Keep good records of your payments and when you paid them.
- Never use ATM machines when withdrawing money from the bank.
- Cut up your credit cards and use cash only.
- Pack your lunch for work and eat out less.

To join Jonathan Edison's V.I.P. club, simply go to **www.jonathanedisonspeaks.com** and leave a **private message** on the guest book. By joining, you will enjoy many amenities:

- Private invitations to upcoming events
- Personal invites to all book signings
- Free motivational materials/updates
- Information on how to stay motivated
- All upcoming news
- Jonathan Edison's own personal newsletter
- Information on any upcoming conference/workshops
- Learn how to get your book published
- And much, much more completely FREE.

All you have to do is log on and leave your name, address, phone number and email address.

Join today FREE at

www.jonathanedisonspeaks.com

Remember, "Success is in your hands!"

To order additional copies of
"How I Became a Millionaire at 30!"
for yourself, church, business,
library or school, simply call
1-800-JEDISON and an operator will
be glad to assist you.

Or log on to
www.jonathanedisonspeaks.com

Call today!

NOTES

About the Author

Jonathan is a young man that is taking the nation by storm as he has quickly risen up to be one of the leading authorities on developing human potential and self-development. He shares his success strategies with thousands of people every year throughout the United States, Africa, Europe, Asia, and Canada.

His speeches are energetic, powerful and life changing. His audiences include Fortune 500 clients and every size business and organization.

Call today for information on booking Jonathan for your next event, meeting, conference or convention.

Jonathan can also customize speeches for keynote addresses, workshops and seminars.

Please visit

www.jonathanedisonspeaks.com

or call

1-800-JEDISON

email: edisonfordetroit@yahoo.com